Crisis at
Santa's Workshop

Crisis at Santa's Workshop

*Using Facilitation to
Get More Done in Less Time*

Richard G. Weaver
John D. Farrell

BK
BERRETT-KOEHLER PUBLISHERS, INC.
San Francisco

Berrett-Koehler Publishers, Inc.
235 Montgomery Street, Suite 650
San Francisco, CA 94104-2916
Tel: (415) 288-0260   Fax: (415) 362-2512   www.bkconnection.com

ORDERING INFORMATION

Quantity sales. Special discounts are available on quantity purchases by corporations, associations, and others. For details, contact the "Special Sales Department" at the Berrett-Koehler address above.

Individual sales. Berrett-Koehler publications are available through most bookstores. They can also be ordered direct from Berrett-Koehler: Tel: (800) 929-2929; Fax: (802) 864-7626; www.bkconnection.com.

Orders for college textbook/course adoption use. Please contact Berrett-Koehler: Tel: (800) 929-2929; Fax: (802) 864-7626.

Orders by U.S. trade bookstores and wholesalers. Please contact Publishers Group West, 1700 Fourth Street, Berkeley, CA 94710. Tel: (510) 528-1444; Fax: (510) 528-3444.

Berrett-Koehler and the BK logo are registered trademarks of Berrett-Koehler Publishers, Inc.

Printed in the United States of America

Berrett-Koehler books are printed on long-lasting acid-free paper. When it is available, we choose paper that has been manufactured by environmentally responsible processes. These may include using trees grown in sustainable forests, incorporating recycled paper, minimizing chlorine in bleaching, or recycling the energy produced at the paper mill.

Library of Congress Cataloging-in-Publication Data
Weaver, Richard G., 1947–
   Crisis at Santa's Workshop : using facilitation to get more done in less time : help others take responsibility and work together effectively / Richard G. Weaver and John D. Farrell.
     p. cm.
   ISBN 1-57675-279-8
   1. Group facilitation—Fiction. 2. Supervision of employees—Fiction. 3. Teams in the workplace—Fiction. 4. Group decision-making—Fiction. 5. Santa Claus—Fiction.
   I. Farrell, John D., 1960–   II. Title.
   PS3263.E387C75   2003
   658.4'036—dc22   20003057889

FIRST EDITION
08 07 06 05 04 03   10 9 8 7 6 5 4 3 2 1

We dedicate this book to our families,
both biological and those who have come to us by choice.
Your support makes all the difference!

•

For my California family. Each of you know
what you mean to me.

DICK

•

For Twylia, my soul mate.

JOHN

Contents

Preface

The Origins of This Story

It was a bright sunny day when we sat on Richard's patio in Oceanside, California, talking about readers' responses to our first book, *Managers as Facilitators*. While we were pleased to have reached so many, we felt that facilitation could have much more of a positive impact on the world of work if more people used it. How could we get more people and organizations interested in using facilitation? We felt the challenge. Somehow, we had to present facilitation in a new, much more engaging way. The activities and results of facilitation are not dry. They are full of life! It was clear we had to tell a story drawing on our great experiences helping organizations use facilitation to meet their challenges.

The mythical setting of Santa's Workshop gave us a unique opportunity to explore the sometimes harsh realities of the modern workplace. After a while, Santa's Workshop became a very real place for us and we grew close to the characters that work there. As one manuscript reviewer told us, "The story is written so much like things really do happen that it leaves you thinking Santa's workshop really does exist."

What Is Facilitation, and
Why Would Santa Care about It?

As we described very thoroughly in our first two books, *Managers as Facilitators* and *The Practical Guide to Facilitation*, facilitation is defined as "helping people get their work done and improve the way they work together." It's about focusing on the right tasks and building the kinds of relationships that help complete those tasks. Organizations that embrace facilitation value the contributions of all. They believe that collaboration creates better results and that differences among people (well, in this case, elves) is a required part of collaboration. Facilitation makes collaboration work. Through facilitation, organizations achieve results by helping their people express themselves productively and take action.

In our story, Santa has a serious problem this Christmas. Toy production is falling short of demand and his Workshop's perfect record will most certainly be snapped unless his team can come up with a breakthrough. Already the most productive manufacturing facility in the entire world, Santa's Workshop has instituted all of the latest techniques. It has the most modern production and communication technology at its disposal. It even has the magic of Santa and the elves. But the Workshop is still coming up short of its goal and the elves need a new approach. They need everyone to work together like never before. They need facilitation to make this possible.

In this mythical story, you will undoubtedly see some situations that remind you of your own workplace. We think you will have fun relating to the very real challenges faced by Santa's management team. We also hope you will see how the "magic" of facilitation can help you and your organization meet your biggest challenges.

About Santa's Workshop and the Elves

Creating a whole organization populated with characters who aren't human was a challenge. Who are these elves? Of course, we had seen pictures and read stories about Santa's Workshop and the elves. They are nearly always pictured as round little figures with pointed shoes and hats. But there are also more recent, contrasting images of elves as depicted by J. R. R. Tolkien in his trilogy *The Lord of the Rings.*

We decided to research the origin of elves to find out more. Tolkien used Scandinavian mythology as the basis for his elves, but he made some significant changes. He made his elves taller and much calmer.

The elves of traditional Scandinavian mythology are little people who live in the woods. They live long lives, and while they occasionally have interaction with humans, they generally avoid them. These elves are very emotional beings with huge, loving hearts. While they are very affectionate, they also can be very quick to express their anger. Manners and courtesy are important to them, and they can be put off by bad manners or minor faux pas.[1]

The mythology we researched described elves as loyal and very committed to their elfin way of life. These elves can also be mischievous at times and once really angered, can carry a grudge for years. We decided to use these elves of the traditional Scandinavian mythology as the basis for those in our story.

There are a wide variety of Santa myths. A number of countries claim to be the origin of Santa Claus. From Southern Europe to the Arctic, characters give children various treats, many as a reward for their good behavior during the previous year.[2] These stories took on a more dramatic flair in 1823 when "'Twas the Night before Christmas" was anonymously published in the *Troy* (New York) *Sentinel*. This poem, actually titled "A Visit from St. Nicholas," touched the hearts of so many people. Santa Claus immediately took on a much more prominent role in the Christmas holiday traditions. Now he appears to be synonymous with the secular side of the holiday.

Much of the American mythology of Santa's Workshop places it at the North Pole, surrounded by snow and ice year-round. Most European versions of the Santa stories place the Workshop in northern Finland. This is consistent with the Workshop's employees all being elves. It would also make the logistics of obtaining raw materials for the making of presents, especially for wooden toys, much more understandable. In our story, the Workshop was having a tough enough time getting lumber shipments on time. We decided to spare the elves the hassle of shipping wood across thousands of miles. Recognizing all of this, we made the decision to think of the Workshop as being in Finland but not to make any direct references to its location in the story.

The Characters

The elves of this Santa's Workshop are the elves of the ancient myths. For this reason, they all have Scandinavian names, primarily from Old Norse. We made the deliberate decision to make the elves the lead characters in the story and have Santa more in the background. We wanted the elves to have to cope with their problems, not depend on Santa to use some of his magic to fix the situation. This made the story feel more consistent with the modern workplace.

We researched elfin names and looked at their meanings. Each of the characters has a name given to connote some important personal characteristic or relationship to the other characters. We used these names to make the story more real for us as we were writing. We hope that you find the names fitting for the story we have created. The names of the primary characters are defined below.

Rune   (secret lore)
Helmi   (strong helmed)
Pekka   (rock)
Emil   (rival)

Santa's Workshop Organization Chart

We thought you would find it useful to have Santa's organization chart as a reference. Most of the story focuses on Rune, Pekka, and Helmi, but the others depicted in the chart below make one or more appearances.

Santa's Workshop
Organization Chart

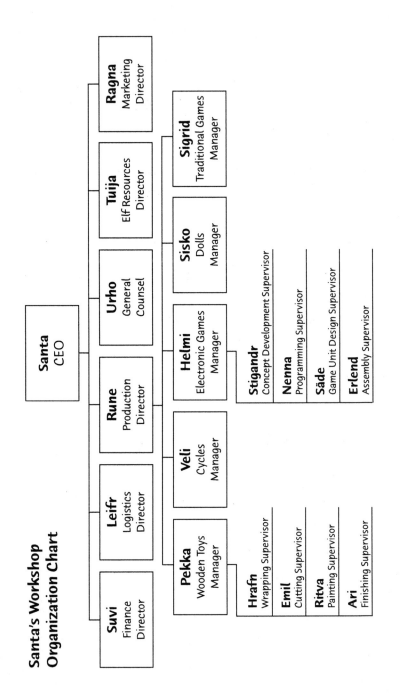

Santa
CEO

Suvi
Finance Director

Leifr
Logistics Director

Rune
Production Director

Urho
General Counsel

Tuija
Elf Resources Director

Ragna
Marketing Director

Pekka
Wooden Toys Manager

Veli
Cycles Manager

Helmi
Electronic Games Manager

Sisko
Dolls Manager

Sigrid
Traditional Games Manager

Hrafn
Wrapping Supervisor

Emil
Cutting Supervisor

Ritva
Painting Supervisor

Ari
Finishing Supervisor

Stigandr
Concept Development Supervisor

Nenna
Programming Supervisor

Säde
Game Unit Design Supervisor

Erlend
Assembly Supervisor

Have Fun, and Try Using This Stuff!

First, and foremost, we hope you find this an enjoyable tale that is full of interesting twists and turns on the way to Christmas Eve. We still have fun reading the story and hope that you will, too. On a more serious note, we hope that you will think about the value of facilitation when you are expected to get work done through other people. We hope you will remember the three basic steps of facilitation:

1. Help others take responsibility
2. Help others focus on what they need to get done
3. Help improve working relationships

A number of resources about facilitation are available. Once you have followed Rune, Helmi, and Pekka through this story, we hope you will want to learn more about the process they used to succeed. We recommend *Managers as Facilitators: A Practical Guide to Getting Work Done in a Changing Work-place* as a good place to start. In this, our first book, you will find a comprehensive description of facilitation that is more complete than any other publication we have found. In it, we present a model that shows how all of the elements of facilitation fit together. We challenge readers to see how in the modern workplace the role of facilitator is now as essential as that of leader or manager. This first book also discusses the subjects of facilitating change and managing boundaries. Finally, in the Quick Fix section, we present solutions to common problems.

The Practical Guide to Facilitation: A Self-Study Resource is a workbook that teaches the reader how to use facilitation and is suitable both for self-study and classroom or workshop settings. This book provides a series of practical exercises that help both novice facilitators learn the basics of the role and advanced facilitators take their capabilities to the next level.

We invite you to visit our Web site at www.facilitation-source.com to learn more and join our learning community that is focused on facilitation. Some content from our first two books is available online and you can also complete assessments focused on facilitation skills and active listening. Coincident with the publication of this book, we will support discussion groups and solicit contributions from site visitors as we seek to build our community focused on facilitation.

Enjoy your time in Santa's Workshop!

Acknowledgments

We write about using facilitation to create a more collaborative environment and we do practice what we preach. The creation of this book has been a work of collaboration. We want to acknowledge each other, the ideas, and the dedication that make coauthoring a labor of love. Our collaboration helps us find and experience the joy of writing.

We also wish to acknowledge some of the specific contributions to this book. The feedback from our first round of readers helped us both realize we were on the right track and identify many areas for improvement: William Randall Beard, Marti Scrivens, Nigel Scrivens, Sarvi Mahdavi, and Yasmine Mahdavi. Our second-round readers helped us refine the story to what you are about to read: Angela Wagner, Jade Stone, Kendra Armer, Irene Flores, and Sara Jane Hope.

Steve Piersanti, publisher of Berrett-Koehler, has our continuing appreciation and respect. He and his staff are a joy to work with. They use facilitation to support their collaborative work environment. We must also recognize the professionalism of Richard Wilson, Dianne Platner, and, always present behind the scenes, Jeevan Sivasubramaniam. Our illustrator, Phil Smith, did a phenomenal job in capturing the characters.

Dick wishes to especially acknowledge Patti Christensen, Telesia Timo, and James Nelson-Lucas for the emotional support that kept him going. Your reviews of yet another draft always resulted in thought-provoking feedback.

John wishes to especially acknowledge Twylia Fannin for the gifts of critical thinking and loving support. Your suggestions inspired me to find the words that gave life to the story. As always, the joy and energy of my children, Brian, Julia, Joseph, Audrey, and Alice, kept me going.

We also want to acknowledge the many individuals who have tried facilitation and found that it does make a difference. You are creating a more collaborative world and helping us pay closer attention to how we are treating one another. Whether you have been using faciliation for years or just recently began experimenting with it, you are the inspiration for this book.

Oceanside, California   Richard G. Weaver
St. Paul, Minnesota   John D. Farrell
October 2003

1

MONDAY

MORNING

25 WEEKS BEFORE

CHRISTMAS

Santa's Management Team

T his is really serious, worse than we've ever seen it before. There are less than 180 days to go. At this rate, we'll disappoint a lot of children this Christmas! I need to hear some good news, *now!*"

The figure standing in front of the conference table looked the same as ever: the full white beard, dimpled cheeks, round belly, and pipe held tight in his teeth. But his eyes weren't twinkling, his belly was not shaking with laughter, and his cheeks were red from frustration, not the cold arctic air.

The six elves sitting around the big conference table looked down as Santa's not-so-jolly voice filled the room. They knew that if children did not get presents from Santa it would be a disaster, not merely a "disappointment." Santa may have used gentle words to describe this crisis, but it was obvious that he was very upset.

For hundreds of years, Santa's Workshop had had a perfect record. Of course, there had been some close calls in the past. Every year production was adjusted right up to

Christmas Eve. And then there was the year when Rudolph had a cold that short-circuited his famous nose. Santa almost didn't finish his ride that night. This year was different. Now they were failing. They knew it. They were far behind in production and slipping further every day. This was easily the worst position they had ever been in.

Santa surveyed his management team with a cold, hard stare. He turned to his most trusted manager, Rune, who had been production director for over forty-five years. "We have less than six months until we pack up the sleigh and I start my annual rounds. Somehow, we must catch up. So, Rune, what is your plan to fix this?"

"I do not have an answer yet," said Rune, slowly raising his eyes from the production report in front of him. The report was splashed in red that didn't reflect holiday cheer. Sitting on the other side of the round table, Rune was uncomfortable as he met Santa's gaze and tried to gather his thoughts. Although he had anticipated Santa's question, he didn't know what to say.

"I do not want to sound like a broken record," Rune said slowly, "but the increase in the production goal this year is beyond our capabilities unless we make some significant changes. For years, we have had to stretch to meet one unrealistic goal after another. It has finally caught up with us. We need to find a totally new way to create a huge leap in productivity. To do that, we have been trying nearly every improvement idea that seemed to make sense. So far, no luck!

"Our raw lumber vendor has short shipped the last four deliveries. We found a bug in our latest electronic game and will have to reprogram over 250,000 units. And our new line of interactive dolls responds only to adult voices, not to the voices of children, who will get them. Add to this the struggles that Elfin Resources is having finding qualified employees, especially for our Electronic Games Group, and —"

"Yes, we know all that," Santa interrupted impatiently. "Wooden Toys is a full 15 percent behind schedule and Electronic Games over two million units below target. This is not acceptable. At this rate, nearly five million children are going to wake up Christmas morning with no gifts from Santa. What in Blitzen's name are you going to do about it?"

Everyone else at the table exchanged uneasy glances. It was normal for Santa and Rune to be in conflict in July. But something was different about the tension between them today. This felt a lot more serious. Rune held Santa's gaze as neither said a word for a full minute. It felt like an hour to the others in the room.

Santa's face softened a little and became closer to his gentle, familiar look. "Okay, Rune, I know your group has increased production by more than 5 percent so far this year. We just need more. I'm thinking about this coming Christmas Eve and of all those children who are counting on us, on *me!* I know you need some additional time to develop an action plan that will put us back on schedule. I will be expecting it in two weeks. We'll all meet then to discuss it. And that leads us directly to those production goals. Ragna?"

Ragna, the marketing director, shuffled through several papers in a folder. Pulling one out, she studied it for a moment as she composed herself. "As you remember, we set our initial production goals based on a linear projection of the trends over the past five years. Unfortunately, those trends don't appear to be holding true.

"For reasons we don't fully understand, children are contacting us sooner and in larger numbers than in the past. Their requests don't match our projections. Listening to them, we now believe the total demand this year will be significantly higher than we had first expected. We are now projecting the increase in Total Present Production to be 6 percent for this season. That is a full percentage point above what we had anticipated for TPP. We are running ahead of world population growth because more communities around the world are choosing to celebrate Christmas in addition to their other traditional holidays."

Ragna paused to look at her notes. "The present mix is shifting, too. Wooden toys have peaked at just over 185 million units, which is 35 percent of Total Present Production. The nostalgia trend in the Western markets has apparently run its course sooner than expected. Electronic games have jumped a full 24 million units from last year, bringing them up to 34 percent of TPP.

"We now must produce nearly as many electronic games as wooden toys. This means that the Elfin Resources Retraining Initiative is going to feel even more pressure. The news about the software bug in our newest electronic game is particularly troubling because, in their early letters to Santa, kids are telling us that wireless multiplayer games are going to be the number one toy this year. It looks bigger than the Tickle Me Elmo craze that nearly buried the Doll Department several seasons ago.

"So, Santa, in answer to your question, I see a couple of added challenges for production. We are going to need more presents than previously planned and the mix is going to be different than anticipated. In short, our latest data shows that the number of children at risk is closer to ten million. Sorry about that, Rune."

"We don't need such a complication this year," said Santa as he slowly shook his head. "Ragna, with things in such flux, keep us posted more often than once a month. And now, Leifr, what do you have to report from Distribution and Logistics?"

Leifr, the logistics director, stood up to deliver his report. "The 6 percent growth in total presents means that we need to make an additional 9 million stops this Christmas Eve to deliver over 525 million presents. Our estimate of 3.2 presents delivered per stop appears to be holding. Our challenge is not raw speed; the warp drive on the sleigh can carry us well into the next decade. The problem is the Time Slice Multiplexor, the TSM. At last year's volume, we were able to set the TSM at 1,800 deliveries per second and meet our goal of 155 million delivery stops. At this year's volume, we will need to achieve nearly 1,900 stops per second. Our current version of the TSM has a design maximum of 1,850 deliveries per second. We hope to be able to tweak it enough to coax it up to 1,900."

"Don't you dare tell me that I'm going to have to go on another diet," Santa joked. It was the first time he had smiled during the entire meeting, and his grin helped break the tension. "There's no way I'm going to drink protein shakes and choke down those horrifying protein bars! A handful of children and adults are going to see Santa this year, as always, and I'm going to be good and fat! I thought we had successfully tested the TSM at 2,400 stops per second in the spring. What's up?"

"Don't worry, Santa. I believe we are going to be able to stretch the current unit one more year. The unit we tested in the spring was a prototype. We are still a year away from using it in our delivery. We won't make you lose weight like we did for the first warp drive conversion. I promise."

Tuija, the Elfin Resources director, spoke next. "As Rune and Ragna mentioned, we in ER have been trying to help solve this crisis. The Elfin Resources Retraining Initiative is gearing up to help retool elves currently working in Wooden Toys and Traditional Games to prepare them for new positions in Electronic Games. Our elves are extremely intelligent and usually are quick to learn new skills. Given the number of changes we have experienced in the past twenty-five years, however, it seems like we are reaching some sort of limit. I can't fully explain it. But it looks like our elves are just plain worn out. Appealing to traditional Santa's Workshop values seems to have an impact on our more experienced employees. But the less experienced elves are challenging the very essence of these values. They are looking for more balance in their lives and pushing back when we ask them to give up evenings and weekends to help out in the Workshop. I see some very challenging months ahead.

"I have to think that one of the solutions we will come up with will be adding to the workforce," noted Tuija. "I can tell you I'm worried about that. Elves are finding other lucrative opportunities. We are still considered *a* premier employer but not *the* premier employer. Many of the best elves are not available to us as they have been in the past. We are going to have to do a lot more training to bring the available elves up to par. My staff is already doing some planning about how to provide the required training, but it would help us if you'd give us as big a lead time as possible. That's all from ER."

"Be careful about solutions that impact our budget too much," remarked Suvi, the Workshop's finance director. "We will be hard-pressed to take on extraordinary expenses, let alone incur a long-term commitment. Make sure you keep me in the loop so we can look at the financial implications of the solutions being considered."

As Suvi finished her input, she looked at Urho, the general counsel. He nodded to her and addressed the group. "As we have been watching the increasing chance that we would not meet our goal this year, I have had our attorneys exploring our legal liability. We have been providing presents to children for so many years that there may be an implied contract that could be enforceable in courts around the world. I believe that we can defend ourselves, but it certainly would put Santa and the Workshop in a very awkward position."

Santa put his papers down on the desk, took off his glasses, and stood up. He looked at each of his six directors.

"I know that you are all aware of the gravity of our situation. I trust you are working as hard as you can to find solutions to these challenging problems. I appreciate your effort. We can't sit back and rest on our laurels from previous seasons. We have to find the answers to these hard questions for this year. Rune, I expect you to present a plan to me in two weeks that will make it possible to produce the needed presents. Obviously, we are going to have to do something quite different from the past. Use your creativity. I am depending on you. The children of the world are depending on you. Don't let us down."

Santa turned and walked to the big rolltop desk along the far wall. The six elves slowly rose without a word and filed out of the room. Rune looked especially despairing as he trudged down the hall back to his office in the Production Center. He felt like he was carrying the weight of ten million children on his shoulders.

2

LATER MONDAY MORNING

Rune Talks to the Coach

Rune's morning had not improved since the meeting with Santa. He'd had a terse conversation with Pekka, the manager of Wooden Toys Production, that left both of them feeling angry and impatient. Thank goodness he was meeting with the Coach in a few minutes. Rune had met the Coach through a management studies program many years ago and had turned to him periodically for help. The problems he faced now were feeling insurmountable and he knew that this work session would help him sort things out. He launched the videoconferencing system on his computer, drew a heavy sigh, and waited.

"Hi, Rune! How's it going today?" The videoconference system blinked to life and there was the Coach's calm, reassuring face on Rune's computer screen.

Rune recounted the events of the day. "This is the first time I have ever felt so at a loss. What am I going to do? If I do not find a way out of this mess, this failure will be my fault. I just do not know how to make this right. Everybody, including Santa, is looking to me to come up with the magic answer. I feel so out of miracles right now! On top of that, I just had a painful run-in with Pekka, the manager of Wooden Toys Production. He went from trying to console me about the assignment to complaining about the problems he is facing. I really let him have it, telling him, 'I do not have time for excuses and you better start hitting your numbers!' He looked at me like I had gone crazy. I just walked away from him. Everything seems to be spinning out of control!" Rune looked as hopeless as he sounded, holding his head in his hands as he poured out his story to the Coach.

"I can understand why that exchange with Pekka was so hard for you. That's not the way you have talked with him in the past. From what you have said about him, I'm sure you can work it out with him once you both have calmed down.

"Now, let's turn back to what happened with Santa. I heard you say that he is expecting you to come up with *the* answer. Is that really the case or just an assumption—your habitual way of doing things?"

The Coach had been encouraging Rune to try using facilitation with his fellow elves to create the needed level of collaboration. He knew that Rune was used to coming up with solutions on his own, but this situation looked to be too complex for his old "direct and delegate" methods. The Coach decided to push Rune to use the facilitation approach that he had introduced.

"Santa is looking for a solution and I do not think he will care about who comes up with it or how it is created.

Unfortunately, the things that we have done in the past are not really options this time." Catching his breath, Rune continued, "When Wooden Toys Production was growing quickly a few years ago, we just added more elves to the staff and expanded the Workshop. Now, we are not able to add staff. Plus, these Electronic Games are a lot more dependant upon new technology. It is not a matter of throwing elves and money at the problem."

"Rune, do you have all of the knowledge and information you need to come up with a solution on your own?"

"You already know the answer to that question, Coach. I need help from a lot of elves. I just do not think we have the time to go through a long group process. Christmas is going to be here very soon and we need some answers right now. With so much going on, I do not know how we could swing a two-day off-site meeting at the Forest Retreat Center." Rune was frowning, the lines on his forehead showing his exhaustion.

"You *definitely* don't need a two-day off-site," laughed the Coach. "I'm not suggesting that. You and your colleagues are extremely creative and capable of figuring this out. Maybe your group can help you figure out *how* to come up with the answers, as well as the answers themselves. I'm sure they have heard about the meeting with Santa by now. They know the time pressure is real. Why not ask your colleagues for some help? They might surprise you."

"The elves are used to me being the one to come up with the answer. They expect me to direct and delegate. How am I going to be able to explain this sudden shift? I am afraid that they will think I have panicked and do not know what to do," said Rune, worriedly.

"Have faith in yourself, Rune. You have made many shifts since you became production director. They understand that. You just need to be confident in what you are doing. Over the past few sessions, we have been talking about facilitation. Let's explore it a little more deeply right now. The definition is a good place to start. Remember, facilitation is defined as helping elves get their work done and improve the way they work together. Your old 'direct and delegate' approach was certainly efficient, but did it put the Workshop in position to capitalize on the collective capability of everyone?"

"Elves have not been knocking down my door with solutions, if that is what you mean," replied Rune. "I know that everyone is looking to me for the next big answer. I am sure they have some really good ideas. I wonder if facilitation could be the way to find our way out of this mess?"

"Let's look at the nature of facilitation a little more closely to help you figure this out," the Coach continued. "Facilitation is about everyone taking responsibility for outcomes, then focusing on the right tasks and building better

---

FACILITATION DEFINITION

Facilitation is a process through which an elf
helps others complete their work and improve
the way they work together.

---

relationships. When Santa's Workshop embraces facilitation, the organization will value the contributions of all elves, not just those from the managers and supervisors. That will be a big change for the Workshop. As we have talked about, facilitation embodies the belief that collaboration creates better results and that capitalizing on the differences among elves is a required part of collaboration."

The Coach looked at Rune as his words sank in. "Rune, you just told me that you can't figure out this one on your own. Santa's Workshop has probably squeezed as much as it can out of the latest technological solutions. Now it is time to look at your workforce for solutions. To complement all the changes that the Workshop has experienced, I strongly recommend you make one more shift: integrating facilitation into everything you do. When you do that, you'll achieve results by helping elves express themselves productively and take action. You remember the key elements of the nature of facilitation that we talked about before?"

THE NATURE OF FACILITATION

Facilitation

- Values the contributions of all
- Believes that collaboration creates better results
- Assumes that differences among elves is a required part of collaboration
- Helps others achieve results by expressing themselves productively and taking action

---

"Of course. It was great philosophical stuff that made for stimulating conversation, but I have a very real, practical problem!" replied Rune. "My elves need something that will make a real difference."

"Rune, that's exactly what I am proposing, something real and practical," answered the Coach. "The first step in the facilitative approach is *help others take responsibility*. You know that having others take responsibility for outcomes is very practical. The approach has second and third steps, but for now I'd like you to focus on this first one. You have stepped forward and been willing to take responsibility for finding solutions. Your challenge is that you tend to take on all of the responsibility. That means you own the solutions that are created. But if others don't take responsibility, too, you will be the only one owning them. Help the others take responsibility for finding the answers that Santa wants. That doesn't mean you stop being responsible for the outcome. It means you engage everyone else to create it."

"Well, you may have a point. We *have* started giving everyone more responsibility for managing his or her own areas right down to the production floor. But we have not really encouraged anyone to take the broader view that I am expected to take." Rune was sitting up straighter in his chair. The fire was returning to his green elfin eyes. "I

FACILITATION STEPS

1. Help others take responsibility.

---

think I can ask them to do that, but I am not sure how they will respond. They are used to me being in charge."

"You and the rest of your team are definitely going to have to start thinking differently about what it means to 'be in charge.' Ask them to join you in solving this problem, Rune. Help them be more responsible. Gather their ideas—get them involved right away. Stay in contact with me as you get this process started."

With a wave of his hand, Rune said goodbye and pressed the switch on the videoconferencing system. The screen flickered once and turned blue. Rune sat quietly for a moment. He now had a direction to go. He was going to take the plunge and use facilitation. Rune picked up his electronic tablet and began to outline how he could help his team take responsibility.

Rune's Production Managers Meeting

Good morning, Rune," said Helmi, manager of Electronic Games, the first of the production team to arrive. "From what I have been hearing, the heat is on! I hope that's what we are going to work on today. Did I guess right?"

"You guessed right on that, Helmi. We really do have our work cut out for us."

Helmi nodded her head, took a seat next to Rune, and ruffled through her papers. Rune reflected how he had come to look to Helmi more and more for ideas and support. She was definitely willing to take more risks than anyone else on the team, a fact that caused others to be wary of her. And she always delivered what she promised, which had created some jealousy among her colleagues.

Veli, manager of Cycles, quietly followed and took the seat to Rune's left. In over 35 years at his position, Veli was a steady performer who could be persuaded to try new approaches with some coaxing. Since he was trusted by the traditionalists in the Workshop, his responses to Rune's ideas and actions had great influence.

In a few moments, Sisko, manager of Dolls, and Sigrid, manager of Traditional Games, came into the room together. Sisko was regarded as one of the wisest elves on the team. She seldom spoke, but when she did, everyone listened attentively. She was an effective manager in one of the Workshop's largest, most complex areas. Rune really appreciated that her Dolls team was only 1 percent under its goal, in spite of the troubles it was encountering with its wood vendor. Sigrid had been responsible for her area for only seven years. Sigrid and Sisko sat together across from Rune, leaving one seat for Pekka.

Since Pekka was usually punctual, Rune was surprised that he was absent when the clock struck 9:00. Rune thought a bit about Pekka, saying to himself, "Pekka has managed Wooden Toys for a long time, even by elf reckoning! The very existence of the Workshop is steeped in the tradition and art of wooden toys. Girls and boys around the world identify Santa and his Workshop with the beautiful wooden playthings that they find under their trees and in their stockings every Christmas. We owe so much to Pekka, and yet times are changing and wooden toys are being replaced by electronic games as the number one toy asked for by children. I wonder how Pekka will weather that storm?"

Pekka arrived a full five minutes late. His face and ears were beet red and he was sporting a sullen expression. He usually sat at Rune's right hand but was forced to shuffle around the table to sit in the remaining seat. He noted with alarm that Helmi had taken "his seat" and quickly looked down at his papers rather than greet his colleagues. Everyone noticed this elfin faux pas.

Rune looked around the table and felt a wave of admiration for his managers. He was pleased to work with such a talented group of elves. "My fellow elves, you know why we are here. It seems that we are in the middle of a reindeer-dropping storm and we have run out of helmets." He hoped to break the tension with a little humor, but only Veli smiled. "They are more uptight than I thought," he said to himself.

"The purpose of this meeting is to start the process of finding a new solution to our production problems. Santa is beginning to put some serious heat on us. He and I met for breakfast this morning and he was actually talking about what it would mean to the Workshop if we skipped some households this year." With that, the tension in the room wound as tight as a bowstring.

"Santa told me, 'Rune, I know this sounds extreme, but if I miss five or ten million children this year, that will have a ripple effect all over the world. Young children believe in me. My presence in their lives helps them be aware of bad and good. I help them think about how they treat other people— even how they think about others. My arrival every year confirms their faith in the power of love and the magic that is created in giving. They carry this faith into adulthood.'

"My good elves, Santa is concerned that we may be responsible for undermining the power of love and the spirit of giving in an already troubled world. I agree with him that our elfish existence depends upon the strength of that spirit. A world that has abandoned love and giving will have no need for Santa's Workshop."

Every elf in the room seemed to have stopped breathing as Rune's words sank in. "I do not know how we are going to reach our goal. I do know that I cannot come up with the answer all by myself. I am sure we can solve the supply and technology problems in front of us. We always do. Everyone has always rallied to find an answer to each challenge. But it is clear that this problem is larger than that. Our elves are troubled in their hearts. I see it in the way they work. They look like they are trapped at their benches rather than feeling joy in what they are doing. I even see it in their informal times together. They just do not have any bounce to their steps. It is our duty as their leaders to help them find a way to be successful. Our very existence as an enterprise, and indeed the well-being of the world, depends upon us.

"Let us take a look at the latest numbers. They continue to get worse. Pekka, you are going to have to set production records in the last five months of the year to make your goal. And Helmi, you, too, will have to set a whole series of new records every month from here on. Of course, you both have been doing that for five years in a row so I expect you will figure it out. I have the new quotas for all of you in this report.

"In the face of this bleak picture, I do not believe that we will find our big answers in the places we have looked before. We have been talking over the past year about handling responsibility differently, and now we are going to have to do it. Trying to work harder using our current methods is going to cause us all to have a meltdown. Instead, we are going to have to agree to work together and take responsibility for coming up with a solution. So I am asking each of you right now to step forward and take responsibility for helping me and helping each other."

Pekka's already sour expression grew worse while Rune was talking. He was still stinging from the abrupt end to their conversation yesterday morning. "You can talk all you want about taking responsibility. I'm behind because I don't have the trained elves and floor space I need. And if you don't come through with the staff and production space I asked for, we can kiss our perfect record good-bye. This isn't about some idealistic, feel-good management philosophy. It's about giving me the tools I need to get the job done. Don't set me up to fail, Rune!"

Rune felt his neck muscles tighten in response to Pekka's comments. "I met with Santa and ER this morning. We are hiring forty more elves, but none of the positions are supervisors. We agreed that if we were going to add elves, they would be producing presents. We are probably going to have to rethink our supervision model."

The skin on Pekka's face turned candy cane red. "That's crazy! Do you want me to produce a lot of *quality* toys or just a bunch of junk? We aren't going to get much production out of these new elves without proper supervision."

"We've found a way to work with a lower supervision ratio," Helmi jumped in, "and have found that the new elves in Electronic Games are doing fine."

"It's a waste of time to compare Electronic Games and Wooden Toys—the two areas are nothing alike! Save your comments for things you actually understand!" snapped Pekka. "You are further behind your goal than I am with mine."

Helmi leaned forward and looked directly at Pekka, her gaze boring into him like two lasers. "We're behind because of a software bug. Once Development fixes it, we'll be back on goal within two months. We have demonstrated that we can increase production by double digits every quarter. A big part of that is our supervision model. I wish you'd just look at it and see how to adapt it to Wooden Toys. Rather than fight about this, why don't we work together and figure it out?"

"How in the tundra can we even consider making an organizational change at the most critical point in our production season?" screamed Pekka. "We know exactly how to increase production in Wooden Toys. I gave you the staffing plan months ago! For every fifty thousand more toys that we produce, we need to add one elf. You have taken away 120 of my best elves and given them to Helmi. That's like taking away six million units of production. Giving me back 40 elves still leaves us short. Why don't you give us the elves, give us the space, and get out of our way?"

Sisko spoke up. "Pekka, we have ridden that reindeer into the snow. You are not going to get more elves because they aren't available. We are going to have to do things differently. In Dolls, we're trying a lot of new things, including different supervision models. It *is* possible to figure this out."

The elves looked uneasily from face to face around the table. The anger had shocked all of them. Tempers had flared before, but not with such deep feelings. Sisko's intervention had capped the explosion for now but everyone knew it would erupt again.

Rune had watched and listened as his managers struggled. It was now time to shift this discussion. "My friends, I really need us to explore ways that we *can* reach our production goals given the constraints that we face. With the exception of Electronic Games (because their demand continues to skyrocket), everyone will have fewer elves to do the work, driven in part by budget limitations but also by lower availability of qualified elves. We also have fewer qualified supervisors to direct the work.

"This is the reality we have to deal with. Wishing it were not so will not change it. We simply have to operate differently. As your leader, I am asking you to work with me to use a new approach: it is called facilitation. I define facilitation as 'helping elves get their work done and improve their relationships.' Using this new approach, we are going to get more elves involved in helping us define a plan for reaching our goal. And it starts with this team. In the past, I have been the primary architect of the solutions to our problems. This time, all of us will collaborate to produce this plan for Santa. My friends, this is not a brand-new management philosophy. We have been getting more elves involved in decision making for several years now. We are just going to be more focused in our approach." Rune

explained more about the nature of facilitation and then
returned to the first step in the process.

"The first step in facilitation is *taking responsibility*. By
this, I mean that I need each of you to really throw your-
selves into this assignment. Put your best thinking into this
problem. How did we come to be in this position? What
factors are contributing to the problem? What will it look
like when we have a solution? What will be happening differently? I'll know you have taken responsibility when you
have answered these questions and come up with a few questions of your own.

"I am asking each of you to join me and take responsibility for producing this plan. Santa has given us a challenge. We are expected to present a way out of this mess in
less than two weeks. I want each of you to think more about
this and bring me your ideas tomorrow at 9:00. Now let us
get out there and move things forward today."

Rune waited until his team had silently filed out of the
room before he started to gather his papers. As he pulled
the notes together, he tried to corral his racing thoughts
and feelings. Rune was deeply disturbed by the confrontation between Pekka and Helmi. He feared that his effort to
rescue the Workshop was dying before it even started.

4

**LATER
TUESDAY
MORNING**

Rune Recruits Helmi and Pekka

Rune checked his messages in his office, thinking about his next move. After excavating his e-mail in-box, he walked over to Helmi's office. It was time for him to take action to lower the tension and help his team focus. The two elves that he most needed working together, Helmi and Pekka, were now the furthest apart. That had to change! Rune knocked on her doorway.

Helmi rose from her chair and invited him into her office. "Hi, Rune. I thought I might see you about now. I was trying to be helpful at the meeting, but I'm sure Pekka was offended by what I said. I swear, he and I are like fire and ice."

"Well, you did put him on the spot. But what you said had a lot of truth to it. I need both of you if we are to find a way out of this mess. More than just your ideas, I need the two of you working together. Both of you can learn from each other and we need a combination of your ideas if we are going to succeed. I heard you invite Pekka to work together. I am here to reinforce that. Will you cooperate with him if I ask you?"

"Of course!" Helmi exclaimed. "I'm getting really frustrated with how slowly we all respond to those rising quotas and changes in our workforce. We have to face facts. Things are changing, and we must learn to be more flexible and adaptable. We are going to have to transform ourselves in order to maintain our place in the world. I assume that will take my working more closely with Pekka—and everyone else for that matter."

Helmi took a long breath as she composed herself. "You know, I'm an elf, too. I'm not the enemy. I have lived with traditional elfin values and practices all my life. They are just as important to me as they are to Pekka. I also realize that elfin and Workshop culture don't welcome change. My fear is that our resistance to change will prove to be our undoing this year. I just can't imagine failing at Christmastime. I believe that mission has become incorporated with our very DNA. I wonder what price we would pay if we lost that and withdrew into the forests."

"I am grateful for your commitment, Helmi. You and Pekka manage nearly 70 percent of the toy production in the entire Workshop. If you two set a good example, then the rest will follow suit. I am asking you to co-lead a project with Pekka to look at everything we do in the Workshop and decide what needs to change and what needs to remain the same for us to reach our goal. This will be a very big undertaking."

"Given what just happened between the two of us, how do you expect me to co-lead with Pekka?" asked Helmi.

"We cannot afford to have you two fighting. I need you to put the needs of the Workshop above your personal differences. That is part of taking responsibility. You are a key leader in this effort, and I need you to step up your leadership skills. Please do not bait Pekka with your comments. You know he has a volatile temper, even for an elf! I am going to support you two in doing this. You will be provided the tools you need, including my time and facilitation skills. Can I count on your effort?"

"Okay, Rune. I know you're right. I'm honored that you asked. I'll do it. What's next?"

"Right now, I am going to talk with Pekka about this project and get his commitment. I will get the three of us together in the conference room tomorrow at one o'clock."

The two managers shook hands and Rune left the room to find Pekka. A few steps from Pekka's office, Rune could hear Emil's raised voice. Emil, Wooden Toys cutting supervisor, was obviously on a roll. "The elves who set those quotas don't understand what it takes to make a fine wooden toy. My workers are becoming so concerned with making the numbers that they are beginning to make mistakes. We are caught in a bind—do we reject a blank cut for a hobbyhorse because it doesn't meet specs or do we use it because we are behind? Quality is our strongest, most treasured value. Now, in the rush to crank out toys, we risk losing it. And what about safety? We've never injured a child and we sure aren't going to on my watch."

"We certainly will not injure any children if they do not get a toy in the first place!" Both Pekka and Emil nearly jumped out of their boots when they heard Rune's voice. "I know this is hard. But I really need you to put your heads together and figure this out. Pekka, when you and Emil are done talking, I have something important to discuss with you. I will wait in your office."

"Okay, Rune. We were just finishing. Emil, I'll catch up with you again this afternoon."

As soon as they settled into his office, Pekka gave Rune a contrite look. "I want to apologize for my behavior at the meeting today. I was out of line."

"Thank you, Pekka. I accept the apology. I must admit I was taken aback by the way you acted. Yes, we all are feeling the pressure. I know Helmi came on strong, too, but that is no excuse for hammering on her. I need to tell you that I expect you to be more respectful of me and your fellow managers in the future."

"I'll try to act more respectfully, but I can't say that I feel more respectful! The fact is that I meant what I said to Helmi. She does get all high and mighty sometimes. It really grates on me. I also think she gets into some very crazy thinking and influences you to think that way, too. You may not like hearing that, but it's what I believe."

"Pekka, we have worked together for a long time. I know about your temper. This is not the first time it has exploded, just one of your more energetic displays. Part of taking responsibility includes being a role model as a leader. You can do better than what you demonstrated at our meeting today. Let us see more of the skilled leader that you are. I know that you are absolutely committed to the success of the Workshop. I value your knowledge, experience, and unique perspective."

"I appreciate that. But, if you value my perspective so much, then know that I fear you and Helmi are taking the Workshop in a very dangerous direction. You talked in the meeting of the risks to the Workshop. Well, I think making big changes right now will jeopardize the livelihood of thousands of elves and even our very existence as an organization."

"Pekka, those concerns are exactly the reason I need your help. I talked earlier about our needing to take responsibility for working this out. I need you to help create a solution rather than sitting on the sidelines complaining about every new thing we try. Santa has demanded we create a plan in two weeks that will outline how we are going to solve this problem. We need the best minds in the Workshop focused on this and we need the commitment of our most influential leaders. That means you. We need your wisdom and perspective to ensure that we keep those aspects of the Workshop that are essential to our success. We cannot just do more of what we have done before. We know that is not going to get us to our goal. I am asking you to serve as co-leader of an effort to ensure that we reach the goal for this Christmas. This is the most important initiative at the Workshop."

"It would be hard to say no to that assignment. Who is the other co-leader?"

"Helmi."

"Well, you found the reason for me to say no. How do you expect me to lead with Helmi when I can't stand being in the same room with her? Find someone else. I'm not going to do it."

"Pekka, how can any of us expect the Workshop to succeed if I cannot get you and Helmi in the same room? If you two cannot work together, then we are doomed! We might as well stop the effort right now and save the energy. I believe that the two of you, along with your key supervisors and some of your workers, have the knowledge and skill needed to pull this together. We have to look at the essence of yours and Helmi's positions to find the answers.

"Pekka, this is not one of those 'voluntary opportunities.' I cannot force you to like teaming up with Helmi, but I am expecting that you will fulfill your responsibility to the Workshop. Put your personal feelings aside, and put the good of the Workshop at the top of your list. The organization needs you on this task. The answer lies in combining your position and Helmi's. I believe you can find it."

Pekka felt completely overwhelmed. He was having a crisis of conscience. Would he be selling out his beliefs by throwing himself into this assignment? Or would he be better able to defend what he felt was important by being a part of the project that would change the Workshop? Was he simply being taken advantage of? How could he fulfill his responsibility? Pekka realized that Rune had hit the key point: they both believed in the mission of the Workshop— to get Santa ready for Christmas Eve. It made a difference that Santa was asking for this plan. But what about all the elves who looked to him to protect their values?

"Is there any chance that the co-leader could be Sisko instead of Helmi? She and I work together much more effectively."

"Pekka, you and Helmi are my strongest managers. And you have the greatest differences. You manage nearly 70 percent of our total production. We need your skills, knowledge, and differences of opinion in order to tackle this project. So many of the things that make you resistant to working with each other are the things that we have to deal with across the whole organization. When you two figure it out, the rest of the Workshop will follow."

"Where do you fit in with all of this? You've always been the one to come up with the answers in the past. Are you just shoving this off on Helmi and me because you think we're not going to make it? Are you just trying to save your own skin?"

"No, Pekka. This is part of my effort to change, too. Rather than simply telling you and the others what to do, I am using a facilitative approach. Key to this approach is a belief that collaboration produces better results. I need you and Helmi to collaborate. The fact that you two often disagree is a good thing, believe it or not! Facilitation assumes that differences of opinion are required."

"Well, we certainly have that part down," exclaimed Pekka.

"Yes, you do," replied Rune. "What I need from you is a more respectful tone toward Helmi. And I have asked her for the same. This is part of what I mean by *taking responsibility*, the

first step in the facilitation process. I am surprised that we
have managed to be as successful as we have, given the 'us
versus them' attitude that increasingly seems to prevail
around here. I am convinced that we need to co-create a new
way of getting things done. This is about productivity, to be
sure. But it is also about how we work together. My role is
going to change. I am not the 'answer elf' any more. I am
going to be a leader who helps unleash the creative potential
of all of us. I have some new ideas that could help Wooden
Toys over the hump."

Pekka saw a familiar look in Rune's fiery green eyes. He
knew that his boss had found a new way to reach a challenging goal. Pekka drew a deep breath and quietly said, "Okay.
I'll give this a try. I am not nearly as convinced as you seem
to be that this is the right move. But I am willing to try. So,
what's next?"

"The three of us are getting together tomorrow to talk
about that. Come to the conference room at one o'clock.
Thank you for giving this a chance, Pekka. It is going to
work out. You will see."

Rune left Pekka's office feeling optimistic for the first
time in weeks. His heart actually felt lighter. He could feel
a smile creeping onto his face. A first, major part of the
puzzle was now in place. Then his smile slipped away and
his brow creased. Thoughts of the enormity of their task
came flooding back to him and threatened to sap his remaining energy. He continued back to his office to get
ready for the meeting with Helmi and Pekka.

5

WEDNESDAY

AFTERNOON

Rune Meets with Helmi and Pekka

A meeting of Pekka and Helmi will be like a couple of big polar bears on the same ice floe," muttered Rune to himself as he sat in the conference room waiting for them to arrive. "I wonder if I will be the bear tamer or an early dinner? They have agreed to take responsibility, so that is a good start."

One o'clock arrived and both Helmi and Pekka reached the conference room at the same moment. They had responded to the call. Now that they were actually in the same room, each was having doubts. They both felt a sense of wariness; their adrenalin was pumping, the old animosity surfacing.

"Thank you for committing to this project," Rune said, with a very serious expression on his face. "Each of you agreed to co-lead the project to review the processes we use in the Workshop to produce presents. The outcome of this review is a set of recommendations for changes that will help us achieve our production goals. The first step in our work is to create a plan that we will use to complete the evaluation and produce the recommendations.

"I told you that I would be using some of my new facilitation skills to help you in your process. One of the keys to facilitation is using your differences as assets. For the next hour, I want you to work together to decide on a recommendation on what is to be included in this project. As you do this, focus on how you can use your different ideas and experiences for the good of the Workshop. Think about how you can find opportunities in the differences rather than reasons for failing. I will leave you two alone for a while to work on this and then check back with you. Any questions before I go?"

Both elves slowly shook their heads. Rune rose to his feet and quickly left the room. Pekka and Helmi sat for a moment looking at each other in stunned silence, wondering who was going to get the ball rolling. They also were a little confused. They had thought Rune was going to facilitate the discussion, but he had just abandoned them.

Helmi took the plunge. "I assume that you are as anxious as I am about this meeting. We haven't been the best of friends."

"You got that right, Helmi. I have no idea how we're going to work together."

"At least we can agree on that. I'm struggling with the same thing," replied Helmi. "For the past year, it seems that any time I put an idea forward I could count on your not liking it, dismissing it as bad for elves, or just calling it stupid, just like you did at this week's managers meeting."

"Wow, let's not bring that up again, or we can stop this meeting right now. During this past year, it seemed like *you* trashed everything *I* proposed."

"Pekka, I guess the reality is that we don't like each other much, but when Rune asked us to take responsibility, we agreed to work together on this project. We know that he chose us because we manage the two areas that make up most of the present production and, therefore, carry most of the risk. Of all the managers, our views are in the most opposition. We know that we will disagree about nearly everything. Somehow, we have to find a way to cooperate, even collaborate. Let's try to get started."

"Okay," Pekka responded. "When I think about the areas to explore, I think about them in terms of how we are functionally organized and the way work is done. We should examine these again and find possible improvements."

Helmi thought for a moment. "We've studied those to death over the past few years. We have wrung out about as much as we can from the way we currently organize our work. We need to look at things at a much more fundamental level, such as our work flows. We are structured right now by functions. I think that may be contributing to our problem. We have to step back and take a more critical view or we will just reinvent the sleigh."

"No wonder you make me so angry! As soon as you say 'fundamental,' I know that you are ready to trash everything, and we've only just started," said Pekka. "I want to talk about fixing things that can be improved and you want to throw everything out and start with a clean slate. You just want to rip up the structure that has worked for so long and put something new in its place. I will not be a part of that. That's not what I signed up for."

"I didn't say 'rip up the structure,' Pekka. I said that we need to rethink the current functional alignment. What good does it do for me to put out new ideas just to have you trash them before we get started? We've got to do something more aggressive or we won't catch up with our quotas."

Pekka sat in his chair with his lips tightly drawn, shaking his head. "This is too much. I can't do this. You're expecting me to do the very thing that Emil has warned me about— dismantle the Workshop as we know it. I can't do that! We might just as well go back to Rune now and tell him. Since we have just demonstrated that we cannot come to any real agreement, having us in charge of this won't work."

"Don't give up so quickly, Pekka," Helmi said sharply. "We have only begun to talk about this."

"We may have only started, but I can see your agenda and I won't be a party to it. It's better to stop now than waste our time."

"If that is what you believe, you get to be the one to explain this to Rune."

"Fine."

Rune Talks to the Coach

O h hi, Helmi and Pekka. I was not expecting you so soon."

"Rune, you're not going to like this. Helmi and I have just met and I thought we were off to a good start and then everything crashed and burned. This is not going to work. We can't even agree on where to start."

"Sit down for a moment and tell me what happened. I want to make sure I understand how things fell apart."

The two managers sat down and gave Rune a quick summary of what they had done and how they had gotten stuck. He periodically asked questions but mostly listened.

"I think I am getting a better understanding of what happened now," said Rune. "You both agree that you want me to decide on the scope of the project. Right now, it appears to be a choice between the extremes of dismantling the Workshop or doing more of the same old things."

Pekka nodded. "Yes, I guess that describes our arguments."

"Okay. This deserves more than a snap decision. I need to think about all that you have presented to me before I decide what to do next. Please come back to the conference room at 2:30."

They both agreed and left the office, separately, each convinced that the other was simply too stubborn to work with. Rune was thrown into a whirlwind of thoughts and fears. Rather than taking a big step forward, the process had actually gone backwards. He could see positions within the Workshop were becoming even more rigid. He had visions of a runaway sleigh heading for disaster. For a moment, Rune sat at his desk with his head in his hands.

"I cannot figure this out alone," he said out loud in the empty room. "I am getting some help."

Rune launched the videoconferencing system and placed an emergency call to the Coach. He was not available, but his secretary said he would return in a few minutes.

Rune tried to gather his thoughts while he waited but felt panic growing inside of him. His high hopes of a few hours before had disappeared in a fog of fear. The videoconference system buzzed, and a moment later the Coach's face appeared on the screen.

"Rune, I hear you have an emergency. What's up?"

"Thanks for calling me back so quickly! I am afraid that we took a step backward a few minutes ago and I do not know what to do next. After we talked on Monday, I took to heart what you said about being responsible. I used that approach to get Pekka and Helmi to agree to co-lead a project to get us out of this production mess. At first, neither of them wanted to work with the other, but in the end they agreed. They met this afternoon for the first time. I made a big deal again about their taking responsibility. I then asked them to recommend the scope of the project to solve our production problem. I even suggested they use their differences as assets, just as you and I had discussed. A half hour later, they were in my office telling me they could not work together. They agreed to come back in an hour to talk with me again, but I have no idea how to get this project back on track."

"Let's slow down a bit and look at both the process you followed and where their cooperation broke down. Do I understand correctly that you talked with each individually, talked with them about taking responsibility, and gained their commitment before you met with the two of them to confirm their assignment?"

"Yes. That is what I did."

"Good," commented the Coach. "Under the circumstances, I think that was a good strategy. That gave you a chance to address their individual concerns before making sure they both heard the assignment.

"Now, let's look at what happened next. I am curious about how you felt when you left them in the room together. Did you leave with a feeling that they were going to be able to easily work things out together? Or did you feel relief that you had passed the responsibility of their working it out together completely to them?"

"I have to admit it was relief rather than confidence," Rune said. "Just before they came into the room, I was thinking about their relationship. They have become less friendly as the years have gone by. Especially this past year, they have almost always stood in opposition to each other. Their relationship has sunk to mistrust and anger. I was feeling extremely uncomfortable."

The coach paused for a moment. "Now that you have had a chance to reflect on your choice to leave them alone, what do you think about it?"

"I blew it. I took the easy way out. Since I did not know what to do, I hoped they would figure it out for themselves."

"I appreciate your honesty," said the Coach. "It certainly is normal to shy away from elves who are at each other's throats. But it looks to me like you abandoned them when they most needed you. They need you to help them work through their differences, not just order them to do so. They are both very capable managers. If they could have worked it out alone, they would have done so long ago. You did well on the first step of facilitation: Help others take responsibility. You needed to attend more to the second step: Help others focus on what they need to get done."

"But I described exactly what result I wanted. I was clear about it."

FACILITATION STEPS

1. Help others take responsibility.

2. Help others focus on what they need to get done.

"I'm sure you were. But helping them focus on what needs to be done requires more than just defining the outcome you want. You slipped into your familiar 'delegation' process. Using facilitation, you also must help them focus on the many intermediate steps that will lead to that end result. You need to ask them questions like, 'What will it look like when this work is done successfully?' and 'What is the current situation?' and 'What are some logical steps we can take to get from where we are to where we want to be?' You can use their desire to get to that end result as motivation to attend to those little steps. As they work on these smaller tasks, they can learn to change the behaviors that keep them from getting things done. You also help them experience a whole series of successes that lead to their accomplishment of the outcome. By leaving the room, you lost your opportunity to help them. Your timing was terrible."

"So I needed to stay with them, no matter how uncomfortable it became. Now that I think about it, I can see that I need to help them slow down their conversations and really listen to one another. This will help them hang in there and avoid blowing up. That sure is a different way of thinking about focusing on the work that needs to be done."

"It is, Rune. You can help Helmi and Pekka learn to be better listeners by asking them to understand each other's position instead of shouting at each other—hoping sheer volume will make the difference. That's going to slow down their conversations and help keep them from spinning out of control. You need the outcome—an agreed-upon scope of this project. To get that result, you'll need to help them change some behaviors—in this case listening to each other. If you focus on the behavior alone, however, they may feel embarrassed and want to give up. By focusing on what needs to get done, you can explore their behavior in that context. Are you ready to give that a try?"

"Yes, I am. And thank you. I stumbled today, and you helped me straighten out my path. I will call you tomorrow morning and let you know how this works out."

"Rune, you are capable of learning facilitation. Your elves have demonstrated their willingness to take responsibility. Now go help them focus on what they need to get done. Good luck!"

As the Coach waved, the screen went dark, and Rune turned his thoughts to his meeting with Helmi and Pekka. He was anxious to get on with it and found himself watching the clock. And then the weight of the whole challenge overwhelmed him. He sat frozen for a few minutes as the goal loomed larger in his mind and his confidence drained.

Then he remembered that the Coach had said to focus on what needs to get done. "I cannot solve the whole problem today. So I will focus on this next step, which is getting ready for my meeting with Helmi and Pekka." He believed now, more than ever, that working with these two managers would get the Workshop moving on the road to success. And he believed he was beginning to see how facilitation was going to help them find the way.

Rune Facilitates Work with Helmi and Pekka

"The future of the Workshop is riding on what we do over the next few minutes." Rune said solemnly. "We each have choices to make. I ask all of us to be thoughtful in what we do and say." Try as he might to prepare for this meeting, Rune felt that the situation was totally unpredictable. Looking into the eyes of his key managers, Rune was startled by what he saw. Helmi's face was ashen. She looked like she wanted to be anywhere but that conference room. Pekka looked like he had just completed a walk to the gallows. He just nodded to Rune as he sat across the table from Helmi. Neither Helmi nor Pekka was looking at the other one.

"I appreciate your both coming back. The last time we met, you described the deadlock you had experienced and told me that you could not work together. You threw it back on me to decide how to determine the scope of this project.

"I have a confession to make," Rune continued. "I let you both down earlier and I need to apologize for my mistake. I have to admit that I was so uncomfortable at the beginning of our meeting that I slipped into my old delegation habit. I gave you an assignment and then left you to work it out. The truth is that I was feeling so much stress that I could hardly breathe. It must have seemed strange to you for me to leave after saying I would help facilitate your discussion. I was wrong. I ask you to give this another chance, this time with me working alongside both of you. We—and I do mean the three of us—need to define the scope of the work if we are going to have any chance of pulling this plan together for Santa by his deadline."

Pekka and Helmi looked at Rune and then cautiously at each other. Clearly, his apology had caught them by surprise. Neither was sure how to respond. Rune sat quietly with the silence filling the room. He was going to wait for one of them to make the next statement. This was another facilitation technique he had learned. He resisted the temptation to fill the silence. His patience soon paid off.

Pekka broke the silence. "Well, I've been doing a lot of thinking since leaving your office. You know that I'm committed to the Workshop. Just how deeply I am committed really hit home with me as I recalled a conversation I had yesterday with Emil. He had heard a rumor that I had resigned from this project and was actually trying to recruit me to lead an effort to stop the plan. I heard my own voice in what he was saying. So even though I'm not sure how to proceed, I feel responsible for helping to solve this problem. I told Emil that there was no way I would defy you, Rune. When I refused him, he stomped right out of the office!

"I feel caught in the middle," Pekka said sadly. "On one side, Emil and his friends want to keep things as they are. They assume that we just need to work harder at what we're doing and we'll catch up. I admit that this idea has some appeal to me.

"On the other side is Helmi," Pekka continued, "who wants to bring about major changes, no matter what the cost. I think that quality and craftelfship are unimportant to her. I believe that she feels the ends justify the means. Since our mission is so important to me, I admit that there are aspects of this thinking that I support.

"In my heart, I am not at either extreme. Our values are precious to me. At the core of the Workshop is the commitment to provide presents to children. I know that we have to make many changes, probably some very significant ones. I'm now coming to accept that. I just will not allow us to randomly change things without an awareness of the possible consequences, both positive and negative. But I'm willing to hang in there."

As Pekka was talking, Helmi felt her body become more and more tense. "I committed to this project because I thought it was so important! I did not feel reluctant; I felt enthusiastic. Well, I can tell you my feelings have changed!

When Pekka's and my meeting fell apart earlier, I felt like the last great hope for the Workshop was dashed. I didn't feel that Pekka was really interested in listening to me or doing anything differently. When I didn't appear to agree with him, he threw up his hands and gave up. I'm still angry about that.

"Rune, you ask me to work with this elf who has insulted me in front of others. Being around him is like being on a toboggan run through the forest. Just when we are on a smooth place and I'm beginning to enjoy the ride, we head for the trees! So here we are on a smoother place and I am tempted to become engaged again because of what he just said. But I know something bad is coming. I don't know when or how long we will go before it happens, but it will come. I am as committed to our mission as anyone in the Workshop. But, Rune, when you ask me to work with Pekka on this project, I hear a booming voice in my head that says, 'Don't be stupid!'"

Rune had been listening thoughtfully to both of his managers. He had anticipated another roadblock and now it was here. He took a deep breath.

"As I said earlier, I need both of you on this project if we are to reach our goal. It is the very differences that you experience that make you both valuable to what we are doing." Rune paused, looking at each of them. "Both of you just said again how important the Workshop's mission is to you. We have to have all the presents Santa needs ready for him by Christmas Eve. I have asked you to take responsibility for our successfully fulfilling that mission. We need to focus on the specific tasks that will get us there. We cannot ignore the ups and downs of our working relationships. Obviously, those relationships are having a huge impact on our getting our work done. I am asking you to focus on the task at hand, which is scoping this project."

"I'm ready to get back on the sled, especially if Rune is going to be with us during the early stages," said Pekka. "We're running out of time. And, Helmi, I'm going to try to treat you better."

"I'll give it one more shot," added Helmi. "No matter how I feel right now, I have to be part of this. Where's my seat on the sled?"

"Thank you," responded Rune. "It is time we focused on scoping the project. By the way, I volunteer to record notes from our discussion this time. Now, Pekka, I would like to start with something you mentioned at the beginning of our meeting. You had some conditions for considering changes to the Workshop. Can you elaborate?"

"Yes. I am willing to make changes after we have carefully considered the probable effect on our way of working. Also, I want alternatives to be considered. I think one of our biggest problems will be determining which actions might actually change our basic way of working and which will simply change behaviors. I expect we will have different opinions about this. At any rate, I'm willing to look at making some changes in how we operate."

"What do you think, Helmi?" asked Rune.

"I can easily agree to that. I think we both care very much about how any changes would affect our elfin way of life here at the Workshop."

"Helmi, this has been a point of contention between the two of you in the past. Please tell us more about how you value our elfin approach to work," continued Rune.

"I'm an elf, too! Of course our way of life is important to me. Quality is everything to me. I still have my grandfather's wooden train set—it was made right here in the Workshop! It is still bright red and black and it rolls so smoothly over the tracks. Pekka, I am sure one of your ancestors made that train. It's beautiful. Quality and craftelfship are at the core of who I am. Being a source of love and generosity in our world is the single most important thing that launches me out of bed every morning. I love the Workshop. It is a key part of who I am, and I know that is true for the other elves here. I don't want to tear it apart."

Pekka sat in stunned silence, trying to gather his thoughts amidst the emotions swelling within him. "Helmi, I have never seen this side of you. Do you really have a train set from the mid-1800s? My father's uncle was the supervisor of trains in those days. I would dearly love to see it."

"I'd love to show it to you sometime."

"Wow!" exclaimed Pekka. "Helmi, I really had you pegged wrong. It turns out that we both really love quality toys. Let's get to work on the project scope document."

Helmi and Pekka, with Rune's help, continued to explore their differences about the scope of the project. When they slipped into their bad habit of yelling without listening,

Rune skillfully intervened. At one point, he said to Pekka, "Before you argue against what Helmi just said, tell her your version of her position." Pekka was forced to define Helmi's position to her satisfaction. This slowed down the conversation and ultimately helped them find the common ground in their seemingly "opposite" positions. This "listening intervention" would become extremely important to the large group of elves who eventually contributed to the project. For today's meeting, it made a big difference.

They also looked at their assumptions about the impact of possible changes. They were in the beginning stages of creating a new way to work together. Rune helped them focus on identifying and completing the series of tasks that moved them toward completing a "scope statement" for "The Plan," as it came to be known during their meeting.

As the end of the meeting approached, Rune shared an observation. "Notice that we discovered some common ground here. It turns out that the area where we thought there was the most differences, our sense of elfin values, was the very item that became the foundation for a solution."

"Rune, this was a great meeting!" exclaimed Pekka. "I guess we both can be more flexible. Focusing on what we had to get done helped me listen better. Thank you."

"I agree, Pekka, " added Helmi. "We had a couple of rough spots, but we got through this okay. Rune, as the meeting progressed I came to count on your facilitation to help us get unstuck. There were several times when I thought we were going to crash and burn. But we didn't. Each time you quietly brought us back to task and got us to continue our process when what I really wanted to do was to smack Pekka upside the head. Now that I have actually listened to him, and I feel heard by him, I may actually agree with him in public!"

"I've got to take this scope statement of ours back to my work group," said Pekka. "Based on the reactions I have gotten in the past, I worry about how it is going to be received, especially by those who don't like the idea of more change. I do know that I stand behind this. I will not be trying to sell something that was driven down my throat. I was a party to creating it and I will defend it. From this discussion, I can see that we'll need to create The Plan with input from more than just your team, Rune. My supervisors need to be in on this from the very beginning. Helmi, what do you think?"

Helmi responded, "I will be dealing with my supervisors who are worried that the pace of change is too slow. Some will see our process as too lengthy at a time when rapid action is required. Rather than time wasting, I see our process as thoughtful. I will have no problem standing behind it, too."

Pekka and Helmi looked at each other, shook their heads, and smiled sheepishly. They got up and headed for the door. Rune watched as they left the room, saying to himself, "Facilitation just might be magic!"

Rune Talks to the Coach

I am still having trouble believing it," Rune said when the Coach's face appeared on the screen for their scheduled morning videoconference. "Both Pekka and Helmi are back on board. They were actually able to agree on the scope of the project. And I can see that we achieved this in a different way. They created it with my help. The project scope was written in their words and they walked out of the meeting prepared to describe it and defend it. That is certainly different than before."

"Congratulations, Rune. I am sure that your presence made a big difference. What was it like for you to facilitate this meeting with Helmi and Pekka?"

"What a challenge that was! This was the first time I have really tried to *help* others do their work, rather than direct them. It became fun helping them clarify their words and work through their disagreements. Luckily, they disagreed a lot so I got a lot of practice!"

The Coach smiled. "I'll bet it was hard for you to get out of their way and let them do the work. How did you see it being different?"

"I kept in mind that I was helping them take responsibility. I had to fight my natural tendency to take back that responsibility when they got stuck. I felt that it would be faster to do it myself and give them answers. Also, I kept asking them to focus on the task before them—to define the scope of the project. That was especially hard when their personality clashes kept distracting them from their work. But at those times I would ask a question that would bring them back to the task at hand. In the past, I would have just barked out orders. In this case, I helped them work through their differences. I have to tell you, though, their relationship has a long way to go. It is still a problem. I cannot see them actually achieving the goal without its improving. I did see some hope of that yesterday, though."

"Rune, you have identified the third step of facilitation: Help improve working relationships," responded the Coach. "Now listen carefully. The single most important determinant of an organization's productivity is the quality of the relationships of the elves who work there. Many try to discount the impact of working relationships on productivity, claiming that such things are 'touchy-feely' and not relevant to doing real work. In fact, the opposite is true. You've seen it at the Workshop with Helmi and Pekka. In the past, their relationship made it increasingly hard to get work done. They had to put aside a long list of grievances in order to work together. And your presence as a facilitator made the difference."

"Seeing them experience one another in a more positive way was exhilarating," responded Rune. "And it was exhausting. I have never worked so hard and said so little! I guess overall I feel good about this new role. I am gaining some confidence in it. But I know there is more work to do on their relationship."

"You're right about that, Rune. And try not to worry about how tiring this was for you. With practice, facilitation will become very normal for you. Eventually, you'll find that you are less tired, with more energy available for yourself and your staff. What do you need to do to progress with this new role?"

"I see that it is going to take a lot of practice to make this process feel natural. I still have to remember to use the three steps of facilitation. Today I was paying careful attention to what I was doing and saying. I will be glad when I can do this more automatically."

FACILITATION STEPS

1. Help others take responsibility.

2. Help others focus on what they need to get done.

3. Help improve working relationships.

"You have made remarkable progress in a very short time, Rune. Now, how can I be helpful to you as you prepare for your production managers meeting?"

Rune and the Coach discussed his objectives for the upcoming meeting. They talked about how to use the role of facilitator to keep the meeting on track and moving at a lively pace. They reviewed active listening and brainstorming, two important facilitation tools. The Coach reminded Rune about "listening intervention" and also identified some key questions that he could ask to get the elves to improve their working relationships. He suggested questions such as, "Can you rephrase that question so it does not sound so much like an attack?" and "What happens to your energy for this project when you experience that behavior?" Rune felt well prepared for his meeting as he concluded his discussion with the Coach.

Rune's Production Managers Meeting

D o you think the rumor is true?" asked Veli as she approached the conference room.

Sisko looked at her colleague as they walked. "You mean the one about Pekka and Helmi agreeing to lead the project?"

"Of course!" exclaimed Veli. "After their big blowup on Tuesday, I thought they would never speak with each other, let alone co-lead a project to overhaul our production processes."

"I just hope it means that we are going to solve our production shortfall," Sisko reflected. "I'm worried sick about it, and I'd like to get moving."

As the clock struck the hour, Rune, Helmi, and Pekka walked into the conference room and took their seats. Veli, Sigrid, and Sisko looked at Rune expectantly.

"After the meeting on Tuesday, I spent time talking with Helmi and Pekka about making some changes. I am happy to report that the three of us are going to work together, really collaborate, to find a way to preserve our

Workshop's perfect record. Helmi and Pekka have agreed to
co-lead a project that will evaluate all of our production
processes and identify changes that will help us fulfill our
mission. The first step is producing a plan that will be used
to accomplish that.

"I will not brush over the differences that Helmi and
Pekka have with each other. These differences will continue
to challenge us, but they will also be a source of our solution. Over the past forty-eight hours, we have been working
with facilitation, and it has helped us use those differences to
scope our project. We will continue to use facilitation as we
produce The Plan. We have been using the three steps of
facilitation: first, help others take responsibility; second,
help others focus on what they need to get done; and third,
help improve working relationships."

"Well, we have nowhere to go but up with that third
point!" interrupted Sisko. "Helmi and Pekka were practi-
cally at each others' throats the other day. Do you mean to
tell me that all we've had to do was throw in a little facilitation? It sounds kind of far-fetched to me."

"I know it sounds a little crazy, but this process actually
helped me listen to Helmi, maybe for the first time in
years," responded Pekka. "We actually got the project scoped
pretty clearly. And I can tell you, when we started the meeting we couldn't even agree on the color of the sky!"

"It really is true, Sisko," added Helmi. "I won't kid
you—we have a long way to go, that's for sure. But I can
work with this elf. Go figure!" Helmi laughed out loud and
Pekka actually smiled at her.

"What I have learned about the power of facilitation over these past two days is amazing," said Rune. "Helmi and Pekka have been going after each other for years. But they agreed to take a chance and work with me in a new way. The three steps of facilitation have really helped us get some work done together. One of the most important things we have learned to do is listen to one another. Instead of shouting our opinions at each other, we each try to figure out what the other elf is saying. It sounds almost elementary, but it really does work! If the three of us have made this kind of progress, imagine what we all can do. The way we are going to meet our goal is to use the collective wisdom of all of us to fashion a solution, and facilitation is the key.

"I know the differences that Helmi and Pekka demonstrated are not unique to them. We can expect that elves throughout the Workshop will struggle with their differences of opinion and even focus so much on their fears that they will be unable to work together. The six of us will lead by example, however, and show how facilitation will help us get ready for Christmas. In order for that to happen, we all must be completely honest with one another. So for the rest of this meeting, I would like you all to put your cards on the table. What are your hopes and fears about the Workshop's keeping its perfect record intact this year?"

"I'd like to start," offered Helmi. "One of our elfin traditions has been to be innovative. We have demonstrated our inventiveness and creativity time and time again. I have hopes that we will be open to further innovation. I look back and see a long string of changes that have made us better.

My fear is that some elves will be so fearful about the loss of traditions that they won't be able to innovate. We already have heard about some elves trying to undermine the effort. If we burn energy fighting amongst ourselves, we will certainly fail. The thought of letting down Santa completely freaks me out. I'd rather die, to tell you the truth. I feel like we really need to get moving!"

"I have made my feelings known to all of you," continued Pekka. "I fear that we are going to lose our identity in the rush to change. I feel that the very essence of what it means to be elves in this Workshop is at risk right now. A key to that identity is our high level of quality. I fear that we will sacrifice quality just to hit our numbers. I am afraid we will lose the special feeling that permeates the Workshop—that we really are the best toymakers in the world.

"In spite of my fears, I am going to give this project my all. I know that by working with Helmi, I can make a difference in preserving what is really important. I believe that my point of view will be heard. In fact, it already has been heard by Helmi. We both support keeping quality as a cornerstone of the Workshop. I know that we need to make some changes, but we are not going to destroy the essence of the Workshop in the name of mindless production increases. I have to admit that the rising quotas make me numb! But I hope that we can pull together and pull off another miracle."

Sisko looked around the room and then took a big breath. "I want to take a moment to say 'thank you' to both Pekka and Helmi. Thank you for being willing to set aside your personal feelings for each other. It took courage for both of you to step forward and co-lead this project. It gives me hope that the rest of us can be as courageous. I hope that we will be able to come together in new ways and find answers that have eluded us so far."

"I expect that each of you is going to experience my working with you quite differently in the coming days," added Rune. "I am learning a new role—that of facilitator. I believe that I am going to be more helpful getting our work done. I expect everyone in this room to be learning this role. I will be talking about what I am doing as I do it. As we go forward, everyone will have a chance to practice. One of the benefits from this will be improving the way we work together. We have all the latest tools and technology, to be sure. But the key to our productivity is the quality of our working relationships. And I am not talking about merely liking each other. I am talking about interacting respectfully and considerately. I am talking about making a commitment to one another's success. I am talking about helping one another learn to use facilitation effectively to achieve our goal.

"We now need to change the focus of this meeting from the ways we relate to each other to developing an action plan that will engage the rest of the Workshop in this effort. While we have set the scope of the project, we still need to develop The Plan. It is going to be a series of steps—what by whom by when—that will enroll all of the elves here at the Workshop in helping us boost production and make our goal by Christmas Eve. Helmi and Pekka will lead this discussion."

Helmi and Pekka guided the discussion that followed as the team formulated The Plan. They used the facilitation skills that they had been learning. They helped the group spend a few minutes confirming their understanding of their assignment and how it fits into the Workshop's mission, what a finished product would look like, and how they were going to proceed. There were many contributions when they brainstormed what should be in The Plan. Recognizing that this plan would be a work in progress, they didn't try to get everything perfectly in order. The group set priorities and made some assignments.

As they gathered their belongings in preparation for leaving the room, Veli cleared his throat. Everyone turned to him. "I have watched with sadness as, over the past few months, we turned on each other as the pressure increased. I have been concerned that our disrespectful ways of dealing with each other had become too much of a habit to break. What I have seen here today gives me some hope that we can change our ways."

Rune interjected, "Veli, I am glad you shared your experience of our having turned upon one another in the past. In our old way of working together, you may not have felt it was safe to give voice to your observation. In the new facilitative environment, we need you to speak up. It is part of our being responsible. I know that speaking up can sometimes be uncomfortable for you. But we need you to share with us. Please don't let valuable time slide by if you see us slipping into old, unproductive patterns of behavior."

"I won't, Rune," responded Veli. "I know that facilitation means helping others give voice to their observations and opinions. I promise I'll speak up."

"Thank you, Veli," responded more than one member of the team. Rune's managers smiled at one another as they felt a new energy building amongst them. They left the meeting feeling better about their prospects, and each other, than they had for many days.

10

MONDAY

MORNING

24 WEEKS BEFORE

CHRISTMAS

Rune Meets with Marketing

When Rune arrived at work on Monday morning, he found an urgent message from Ragna asking him to call her as soon as he arrived. He dialed her number and she asked to meet with him immediately—more changes in production quotas was the subject.

Ragna arrived in minutes and launched right into a new production quota report. The numbers had changed again. While the quotas for Wooden Toys remained nearly the same, those for Electronic Games rose another 750,000 units. If the last quotas had been nearly impossible to fulfill, these were going to be immeasurably harder. What a way to start a week!

When he looked up at her, Rune saw that Ragna's forehead was creased and her gray eyes communicated both fear and sympathy. "I'm sorry to have to bring this kind of news to you. This is just phenomenal. We have never had to make such a large adjustment at this point in the year."

"We were still trying to figure out how to reach the last set of numbers you gave us. Now this! Ragna, what is driving these changes? You are making big adjustments nearly every week!"

"I wish I knew! Our best guess is that crossover is causing this. More non-Christian humans are celebrating Christmas. We think that the commercialization of Christmas in areas that have not traditionally celebrated the holiday is contributing to it. We are working as fast as we can to rework our models to reflect these changes. Unfortunately, this won't be the last time we will adjust your quota. We have a changing market that is presently very unpredictable. It's embarrassing that we have not yet figured this out. We realize that you are really under the gun. All I can say is that we are doing our best and we'll keep trying to get this right.

"I advise you to expect an additional increase in Total Present Production, even after this one. The mix will probably change again, too. We also are seeing shifts in where the presents will be delivered, but that is a problem for Logistics. They are having their usual challenges, but I don't sense that it's serious."

"At least Logistics appears to be ready. I only hope we produce enough for them to deliver." Rune leaned back in his chair, put his hands behind his head, and stared at the ceiling. He paused for only a moment. "This rate of change is certainly playing havoc with us. We have been used to things being so much more predictable. What I am hearing you say is that you do not see any reason to believe that relief is on the way."

Ragna shook her head. "I'm afraid not, Rune."

"I guess we are just going to have to get used to this. We'll have to figure out how to be more flexible—how to initiate, plan, and execute while the ice is shifting beneath us. It is like learning to dance on a windblown ice floe."

"Rune, if anyone can teach us how to do that, it's you. I'll update you in a couple of weeks, or sooner if we get new information." Ragna gave him a reassuring smile and left his office.

The meeting with Ragna had been another wake-up call for Rune. These problems were not going away. In fact, they were growing worse. He immediately put in calls to Pekka and Helmi, requesting that they meet with him later in the morning. They had to find some breakthrough and they had to do it fast. His rising sense of urgency, verging on panic, was fueled by the shrinking time before the deadline. He kept thinking of the children on Christmas morning. Rune took a deep breath and reminded himself to focus on his next task, which was helping Helmi and Pekka organize the input that they were currently gathering from their respective staffs.

Pekka Meets with the Wooden Toys Supervisors

Pekka, what were you thinking when you agreed to this bunk about reducing the number of supervisors and putting more responsibility on the frontline elves?" cried Emil, as the Wooden Toys supervisors reviewed The Plan. "It looks like you are selling us out."

In this meeting, Pekka's fears about the reaction of the supervisors were proving to be all too true. Emil had started criticizing Pekka before he had even handed out the document.

As Pekka tried to continue the discussion, Emil took over the meeting by insisting his concerns be discussed. For a few moments Pekka ignored Emil and tried to remember some of the ways Rune had tried to facilitate a solution. He was thinking about how to remind his team members of their responsibilities and how to help them focus on the work before them. He felt so much less skilled than Rune. And he was being consumed by his own anger at Emil's insubordinate behavior.

"Emil, I need you to settle down. All of us must focus on our purpose this morning—to review The Plan. I need constructive criticism of our approach to getting the whole Workshop involved in increasing productivity. Can we commit to fulfilling the purpose of our meeting?" Pekka was on the verge of exploding himself, wondering how long he could hold his own temper.

"See? You're doing it again!" cried Emil. "You are assuming that reducing supervision is the only way to go and you won't even consider my opinion!"

"Emil, that's enough!" Pekka shouted. "I'm interested in your opinions on what we are proposing, not your fixation on something that isn't even in The Plan. Try to sit quietly for the next ten minutes and hear what we are actually proposing at this time. Let's give someone else a chance to talk." Pekka caught himself and calmed his voice, although he could feel his knees shaking in anger.

"Or what?" interrupted Emil again. "You can't get away with this, Pekka! I've been talking with the other elves and they are fed up with all of these changes. We will stop you!" Emil looked around the room for support, but all he received were disturbed looks from his colleagues.

"Emil, will you cool down and at least read through this with us?" asked Ari, the finishing supervisor. "This is only getting us further behind."

"Okay, Pekka," Emil said, with bitterness in his voice. "You win this round. But you won't be able to quiet all the elves who are on my side!"

Emil grabbed his copy of the document from the table and hurried out the door. All of the elves remaining in the room felt the shock of Emil's anger. They sat in silence for a few moments after Emil was gone from sight.

Pekka took a deep breath and started the conversation again. "I'll take appropriate action with Emil after we finish this work session. I know we're all under a lot of pressure, but Rune thinks our working together to find answers is the best way to go. I agree it's our best chance at getting Santa ready by Christmas Eve. Let's figure out how we're going to make this work."

"Pekka, you have been my leader for twenty years," said Hrafn, the wrapping supervisor. "I want you to know that I am behind you 100 percent. I don't really understand what you are proposing, but I'll work at it until I do. If you and Rune think this can work, then I'm with you."

"Thanks so much. You don't know how much that means to me. I was just thinking about something Rune told Helmi and me yesterday, that he is absolutely committed to our success. It strikes me that all of us could really benefit from making a similar commitment.

"One of the changes he is beginning here at the Workshop is the use of facilitation," continued Pekka. "He wants us to help everyone work together better and improve our working relationships. I am learning how to do this and I want you to learn it, too. We can uncover the best ideas and make them even better. He knows that the planning will take a little longer, but we'll pick up speed later because we will all understand exactly what we're trying to do.

"The basic idea is to have elves across the whole organization work in groups to build our plan. The process that Helmi and I outlined offers everyone an opportunity to have his or her voice heard. That includes elves who believe that we should simply continue doing what we have been doing, only better. That seems to be Emil's position. I will want to know how we can do it better. Others want to bring about wider changes in hopes that they will help us be successful. I want us to listen to all of the ideas. Any questions or comments so far?"

"Pekka," said Ari, "thank you for getting this meeting on track. I actually agree with some of the concerns that Emil raised. I definitely do not agree with his tactics. I have something to say about The Plan."

"Me, too," said Hrafn. "The success, even survival, of the Workshop is everybody's business. I understand that this will not be a purely democratic process where every elf will have a vote. But it is important to me that my voice is heard and opinions considered. What I see in this document so far is an intention to give us the opportunity to talk with you about these things. That works for me. I'm interested in our continuing through the document."

"I'll second that!" added Ritva, the painting supervisor. "I also want to tell you that Emil has been busy talking with other elves. While some have rallied behind him and will follow his lead, more have taken a wait-and-see attitude. Everyone is a bit scared and knows that something needs to be done and done fast. Many of us hope that this process will lead to action."

"Thank you," responded Pekka. "I believe we need to foster a climate of freedom to share concerns and ideas about what is happening at the Workshop. Let's go back to the second page of the document. What are your questions about what we are proposing?"

The team had a lively discussion about The Plan. Pekka noted that their concerns aligned with the sections that had been most highly debated the previous afternoon between him and Helmi. He was excited at the quality of the discussion that took place after Emil's departure. He was pleased with his own actions in helping the discussion be richer and more extensive, recognizing how he had helped draw out more comments than would have otherwise been shared. One of his favorite questions to ask his team was, "Have we missed anything?"

With a desire to take this feedback to Helmi and Rune, Pekka left the meeting feeling like facilitation was going to make a difference. They were on the way to completing The Plan on time, and it just might help them make their goal! His confidence in his ability to facilitate change was growing. But he was wondering, "What in the world am I going to do about Emil?"

12

WEDNESDAY

MORNING

Helmi Meets with the Electronic Games Supervisors

I'm relieved that we're finally going to take some action," said Säde, the game unit design supervisor. "I was worried that everyone was just going to keep talking about the mess we are in and no one was going to do anything about it."

"Personally, I am relieved that you and Pekka are finally talking civilly with each other," said Nenna, the programming supervisor. "I could see you two going at it until the whole Workshop came down. This is a major improvement."

Helmi was pleased with her team's acceptance of the challenge of developing The Plan. As she facilitated the discussion, Helmi found her supervisors were really engaged. They did not appear to be threatened by the changes that were sure to come. They readily shared their opinions, and no one was completely opposed to the production of the document and all it implied. They did find numerous areas that they felt needed much more development if there was to be more participation across the Workshop.

"I think we have a good chance of making this work," observed Erlend, the assembly supervisor. "It's great that so many elves are going to have the opportunity to share their thoughts."

"I agree, Erlend," chimed in Stigandr, the concept development supervisor. "But I'm worried about the scope of this project. We are going to have to tackle a wide range of issues. I think we are definitely at risk of biting off too much and then choking on the size of this thing."

"That's an important concern, Stigandr," said Helmi. "Let's spend a few minutes looking at the scope and see if you think it needs to be changed." Helmi helped the group generate and organize its ideas using a brainstorming and sorting process. Her team clearly had an appetite for taking on a wide range of issues, so was less willing to reduce the project's scope.

After that discussion drew to a close, Nenna, the programming supervisor, raised a concern. "We are asking many elves to participate in ways we have never asked them to before. How can we help them speak up and be heard? I worry about the programmers on my team. They are really smart and have some great ideas, but they tend to prefer smaller meetings with fewer participants. I'm not sure if they'll speak up in a large group setting. I wonder how we can draw them out. I don't want to lose their ideas."

The others nodded in agreement.

Stigandr replied, "We don't want to underestimate the capabilities of our elves. We must also remember that drawing out the ideas of our fellow elves is our responsibility,

too. We need to make sure we are hearing what they are saying, and, if they struggle to be clear, we have to help them
articulate what's on their minds."

"Those are good points," commented Helmi. "We will
need to make sure we create a variety of ways for elves to
participate. We can use e-mail and create a Web site where
the quieter elves can submit their ideas. We can have discussion sessions like this one. Plus, I'm going to ask each
of you to take responsibility for working with your teams to
produce a lot of ideas. I have great confidence in your abil-
ities to do that."

Säde stated, "You know, maybe we can get Wooden Toys
to produce a good old-fashioned suggestion box. It might
seem a little corny, but I think it would add some fun. Isn't
it supposed to be fun to make toys? Honestly, the pressure
and the somber faces around here have been getting to me.
We need to lighten up a little!"

The team had a good laugh over Säde's comment.

Erlend spoke up, "Thanks, Säde, for reminding us to
have fun. Unfortunately, I want to bring up something that
is shaping up as the opposite of fun. Several of the elves in
my area reported that they had been approached by Emil
about opposing the process we have just been discussing.
Has anybody else heard anything?"

"I have," said Säde. "A few of my elves were talking with
Emil in the hall. They said they had more confidence in
upper management. Most of them told him to take a hike.
I guess you could say Emil's actions are a distraction when
we need focus."

Helmi had been listening to the discussion, waiting for an opportunity to share her thoughts. "Emil is definitely creating some controversy," she said. "Ultimately, he is hurting himself by what he is doing. I have to admit I am baffled by him. He says that he is not being heard as he takes a loud stand against a process that is designed to let the Workshop hear from everyone, including him. It's strange!

"Pekka actually shares many of Emil's concerns and perspectives," Helmi continued, with a wry smile. "I have found that I can work with Pekka, even though we have some significant differences. You all know that I am willing, even eager, to try new things. I had assumed that Pekka would always be a wall of snow blocking our path. But he's not someone who is simply trying to delay progress. He is just very thoughtful when considering new things. I'm learning from him to slow down a little and look more at the broader effects of my actions rather than just the immediate benefits. At the same time, I think I'm helping him move faster in considering new alternatives.

"This brings up an important point for all of us," continued Helmi. "We're going to hear disagreement. We need to listen respectfully to what our elves are telling us. We want to encourage all of them to share their constructive opinions, even if we don't agree with them. I know that Pekka is dealing with the situation with Emil. Pekka is a very skilled supervisor and is making all of the right moves. Please don't go on the attack against Emil. At this early stage in our learning about facilitation, we do not want to squash the dissenting voices, even if we are concerned about how those voices are being expressed. Give them a little room. We might learn something!

"You have the latest information. You understand the intent of this project and the details that have been developed to date. I urge you to share this with the elves in your areas. Invite them to use the process we are creating. This will ensure that all the elves in the Workshop will have an opportunity to contribute. Keep me posted on any new developments."

As the meeting adjourned, Helmi felt pride in her team—they were stepping up when the Workshop needed them the most. They had taken responsibility and stayed focused on the task and they had solid working relationships amongst themselves. She had always considered them a high-performing team, but today they had surpassed her loftiest expectations. "It's a good thing," she said to the empty room. "We're going to need it."

Pekka and Helmi Meet with Rune

I think I am going to burst!" Rune said to himself as he paced his office. "I cannot wait to hear how things have gone in the team meetings." Questions kept running through his mind. How had their supervisors responded to the draft plan presented to them? What did they like? What were their concerns? Could he count on his managers' teams to pull together? When would his managers ever arrive and report? Rune felt his old, familiar impatience boiling inside. Lately, he had been working very hard to be patient while others carried out their tasks. His anxiety was as high

as ever even though he had less control over the situation
than in the past. He was used to being in the middle of
things, directing the work rather than waiting for reports.
What a challenge!

Helmi and Pekka arrived at the same time and quickly
took seats in Rune's office. They looked at each other.
Helmi nodded to Pekka to start.

"I'm still reeling from my meeting!" he said. "In the
past, I would have called it a disaster. But after talking things
over with Helmi, I realize that we made some real progress."

"What happened?" asked Rune.

"As you might have expected, Emil was spoiling for a
fight. He ranted so much that, at first, it was hard to have a
discussion. He was belligerent and disrespectful. I could
have easily made a case for insubordination and recom-
mended disciplinary action. But I realized that would simply add to the volatility in the Workshop. Somehow, I kept
my temper from exploding. My choice to stay calm paid off.
My other supervisors clearly were annoyed with Emil. When
I confronted him, they stood behind me. Emil made some
threats, grabbed a copy of The Plan, and stormed out of the
room. By the way, I consulted with ER. I will be giving him
a verbal warning.

"Anyway, after we recovered from Emil's outburst, we
really got into The Plan. I worked hard at using some of
the facilitation tools that I have been learning from you. I
especially worked at keeping them focused on the task at
hand. I feel great about my team's contributions. There
were a couple of areas that they really dug into. I think many
of their ideas will improve what we have created so far. I

think their overall reception of The Plan ranged from neutral to positive. I expect each one of them to support it in the end. The only one I am really worried about is Emil."

"Yes, Emil is a challenge," said Rune. "We will talk about that after Helmi checks in."

"My meeting went well. We did not have the fireworks that Pekka had. But Emil had an impact on our meeting, too. The managers wanted to report what he was doing. I, too, had to work hard at keeping them focused on the task before them. They were very receptive to The Plan and refined it. I brought back a lot of great ideas. My concern with them is that they want to go so fast—too fast, I think. Pekka, I've come to appreciate the way you think about these things. I want you to talk with them about the need to balance change with preserving the attitudes that have made the Workshop a special place to work. My team is so often leading in change situations that I want them to learn a more balanced approach. Will you help me with that?"

Pekka responded warmly, "Helmi, I'd like that."

Rune felt a thrill run up his spine as he observed the exchange between his two managers. "Clearly, we need to get more elves involved and share some information about what we are doing and why," he said. "This lack of information will become a huge problem in a short time. I am pleased with the progress that both of you have made. Your meetings went as well as can be expected. What I am most gratified to see is the teamwork that is growing among us."

Rune continued, "We have certainly had a range of responses from the managers—from enthusiasm to cautious optimism to resistance to outright insubordination. I guess that had to be expected. In my naïveté, I assumed, or at least hoped, that if the three of us could work together to develop a useful plan, when we shared it with others they would quickly jump on board. Now that sounds like an overly optimistic scenario. I never considered that our actions to create needed change, even with everyone's help in designing it, would threaten some of the elves enough that they would respond so strongly against us. I am shocked at Emil and equally shocked at my own tunnel vision. As for the extent of Emil's activities, his actions are in direct violation of the charge that Santa gave me last week. If necessary, I will talk further with Santa about what to do with Emil.

"Let us spend the last of our meeting strategizing how we can use facilitation to complete The Plan over the next week," said Rune, guiding them. "We must be as concrete as possible about what we are going to do."

For the balance of the meeting, the three brainstormed ideas and then selected some approaches that they thought would be helpful to use with the elves so troubled by the changes. They explored more deeply the new ideas that had already been produced by Pekka's and Helmi's staffs. At the end of the meeting, The Plan was further developed and they had a strategy for helping the elves who were concerned about the coming changes. At the core of their strategy was an intention to share more information. They contacted Santa and asked him to circulate a memo explaining that the initiative was under way and he was supporting it. By the next morning, every elf had received a copy of the following memo.

– MEMO –

TO: All elves of Santa's Workshop
FROM: Santa
SUBJECT: To reach our goal, we must change

My fellow elves,

As you undoubtedly are aware, the Workshop is at a crisis point. We risk failure in our basic mission, providing presents for children on Christmas. If we continue as we have, we are certain to fail. We must make changes.

I have asked Rune to develop a plan to get us back on track and reach our goal by Christmas Eve. This plan will produce the results we need and preserve what is important to us as elves. That is a seemingly impossible challenge. But I know we are up to it.

Your input is vital to producing The Plan. I have faith that Rune and all of you will be able to achieve this. I ask you to help wherever and whenever you are asked.

Faithfully yours,

Santa

Rune's Production Managers Meeting

D id you read Santa's memo?"

"Did you get to talk to him while he was here?"

"I can't wait to see The Plan!"

"I wonder what they've cooked up?"

Every elf in the Workshop was talking at once.

"I got to help with the part about how to plan the schedule!" exclaimed one of the fore-elves.

"My team gave them some ideas about how we would measure the success of the tasks," added another elf.

"I heard that Emil got a copy of an early draft and said it is a pipe dream," claimed one of Emil's friends. "I don't know why you are so excited. We are probably heading for a disaster."

"I've had enough of Emil's complaining and doomsaying," retorted Hrafn. "Rune has never let us down and I think he is really on to something here."

In fact, several managers and supervisors had been called in to help with The Plan, but only Rune, Helmi, and

Pekka had seen the whole thing. Naturally, the rumors were flying. Tension was rising quickly and matters were coming to a head.

The three had gathered for an early-morning meeting in Rune's office. "It's time for us to formally announce The Plan to our managers," said Rune to Helmi and Pekka. "We need to develop a solid communication plan, and then we can roll this out."

They quickly developed a plan to distribute this important information via e-mail, memo, and word of mouth. They realized that they needed to involve more elves. This time, Pekka and Helmi surprised Rune.

"We've been talking this over, and we think we need to get some input from our staff in order to decide which elves to use," said Pekka. "Our team members can help us assign the elves who are best suited to complete these tasks. Let's get some more elves involved in the project. It will save us time later on."

Rune could see that the team was really starting to support The Plan.

"I suggest that we meet individually with the other production managers—Sisko, Veli, and Sigrid—to share our plan and get input from them," said Rune. "These discussions will help us determine how supportive or combative our colleagues will be." Rune knew that the change process happens at a very personal level. He wanted the potentially controversial information shared in an intimate setting where elves could feel comfortable speaking freely. Studying organizational change had become a big part of his facilitation training. Rune realized he was now beginning to see that practical steps were needed to make change happen. The communication plan and the creation of work sessions where elves could begin the change process at a personal level were two such practical tools.

"I know that we all have been trying to keep up with the cutting-edge approaches used around the world," said Helmi, "but I think we need to make sure we are getting all the new ideas we need. I suggest it would be good to identify a small group that would look again to see if there are some new ideas that we should add to our final plan."

"I can think of one or two elves who would contribute well to such a team," added Rune.

The others quickly agreed and added this group to their plan.

"Before we go rushing out to introduce The Plan to our other managers," said Rune quietly, "we must acknowledge that implementing such a plan will take time away from producing presents. For a time, we will fall further behind. I am willing to accept responsibility for this. I believe that without this effort we will certainly fail. If it works, we will catch up."

Helmi and Pekka expressed relief that Rune had given voice to one of their biggest concerns. They talked it over and agreed that they would acknowledge the expected dip in productivity.

"There is a lot of anxiety out there," said Pekka. "We can help our teams convert their nervous energy into productive output. But it will take a few days at least."

The three then set up meetings with the other managers and planned on speaking with them individually.

"Well, it is out of our hands now." Rune looked thoughtfully at Helmi and Pekka. "You two can cover this plan with your staffs first thing in the morning. Let me know how it goes."

Pekka and Helmi stood up at the same time. "Let's go get 'em, Helmi," said Pekka. They strode purposefully from the room.

Rune spent the rest of the afternoon answering e-mail. Feeling fatigue catching up with him, for the first time in several weeks, he went home before 7:00. "This is odd," he said to himself the next morning after a good night's rest. "I usually have a hard time sleeping when I am this keyed up. Maybe we are going to be all right after all."

When he arrived at the Workshop, however, the news was not good. "So much for my ability to read the future," he scoffed. The daily production report was already showing a more significant dip than he had expected. Elves were obviously talking more and producing less. "I cannot believe it has started already. I hope it does not drop much more than this!" Rune kept himself busy the rest of the morning, anxiously awaiting his staff meeting.

Just after lunch they all gathered in the conference room to review The Plan. They all held marked-up copies of it. Rune walked into the room and called the meeting to order.

"It is good to see each of you here this afternoon. We have a lot to do. Sisko, what did your team think about The Plan?"

"My supervisors were very impressed," she reported. "Actually, they were surprised. They found it much more comprehensive in scope and inclusive in participation than they had expected. A couple of them were clearly relieved. That said, they had lots of comments and suggestions that they hoped would make it better. I'll add them as we go, but I wanted you to know that it was well received."

Veli smiled as he heard Sisko's report. "I'm glad to hear that your group was so receptive. My group's reaction was much more mixed. I had a couple who liked it, a couple who were concerned about how we were going to do it and still produce presents, and one who felt it went too far. I also have feedback and suggestions."

"My group's initial reaction was not positive," said Sigrid. "They looked overwhelmed, to tell you the truth. I tried to walk them through it like Pekka and Helmi did with me, but I felt a little overmatched. It is a lot to digest in one sitting. I will say that their attitude seemed to shift just a little by the end of the meeting. They know that this is a real change and that the Workshop is serious about doing this project. They are worried about our ability to execute, but I know that they will do their part when the chips are down."

Rune, Helmi, and Pekka were inspired by the energy the other three managers were bringing to the process. For the next hour they went through The Plan, point by point, considering the feedback from the supervisors in all five production areas. With Rune reminding them regularly of their task, they hammered out changes. They didn't worry so much about the wording as about getting the ideas right.

Pekka and Helmi made sure they understood the intention of the decisions made by the group and volunteered to clean up the wording later.

They were able to do this through Rune's asking one of his "magic facilitation questions," as Pekka called them. Rune would set up the question like this: "We seem to be getting hung up a little on what words we choose. Let's pretend that we are writing our own dictionary right now. Let's just list all of the ideas, words, and intentions that we wish to convey with this word or phrase." After the group recorded all of these ideas, he would say, "Which word or phrase do you want to use to represent all of these ideas?"

The power of this approach became evident to all the first time they tried it. When they were done with the discussion, the actual word choice was much less important. They had come to agree on the meaning and intention of what they were trying to say. This led to a relatively quick agreement on the choice of words. They finished their work on the document and gave a collective sigh of relief.

"Well done!" exclaimed Rune. "I am really encouraged by the quality of the observations and suggestions the supervisors provided. Going to them for input was good practice for us all. The process we followed in creating this document is at the center of the process we are going to follow to identify what needs to be changed here at the Workshop. If the elves feel good about how we put this together, it should give them hope about what is to come. Helmi, Pekka, and I will put this document into its final form based on the decisions we made here this morning. It will be presented to Santa on Monday morning. I ask that each of you attend that meeting. Your presence will demonstrate that this has been a collaborative process. It will signal the changes that are to come."

"I wonder what Santa is going to think about having all of us crash his meeting?" mused Veli. Everyone laughed at the thought.

"We have work to be done before Monday," said Rune in closing. "We need to revise The Plan and talk with everyone we can about it. I have a meeting with Santa late this afternoon to preview it for him and apprise him of the other developments in the Workshop. Thank you for your time and effort."

15

FRIDAY

AFTERNOON

Rune Meets
with Santa

R une," Santa began. "I know that I gave you a very big mountain to climb when I asked you to come up with a plan that would get us to our goal. We are in deep trouble for this Christmas. You have led the Workshop to higher and higher levels every year. I can tell you here in private that I have been genuinely afraid that this year we would come up short—a failure that would be my responsibility. I appreciate all that you and your staff are doing to avoid that failure. Now, let's look at The Plan."

Rune had felt the warmth of Santa's office as soon as he entered late on Friday afternoon. The feeling was due to more than the cheery fire in the fireplace that radiated heat—there was also a sense of comfort that came from being close to Santa. Rune thought to himself, "I still get excited by him, after all these years. I remember the first time I met him—that feeling of awe and wonder has never left me."

In the quiet of Santa's office, Rune was able to step away from the pressures that he had been feeling. He knew and trusted Santa. As Santa's warm welcome melted away Rune's tension, he began to believe again that anything was possible.

"The team has done an outstanding job on The Plan, Santa," Rune began. "The process has hit some bumps, to be sure, but I have confidence in this approach. Some aspects of The Plan are new for the Workshop, but I would like you to give them a chance to work." Rune outlined The Plan, highlighting the process that the team had followed. He gave Santa an honest accounting of what had transpired over the past two weeks at the Workshop.

Santa asked very perceptive questions that demonstrated his insight into organizational dynamics in general and the particular ones of the Workshop. After Rune had answered each of the questions, Santa got a twinkle in his eye again. "Rune, you seem to have mastered much about helping all the elves take responsibility, focus on what needs to be done, and improve their working relationships."

Rune sat momentarily with a shocked look on his face. "Santa, why not just tell me to use facilitation? You obviously know a lot about it, even the particular steps I have been working on. Why wait for me to discover this on my own?"

"Rune, the most important lesson I have learned in my decades of being Santa Claus is to help people discover their own truth, not prescribe it. When I saw you get interested in facilitation, I decided to teach myself about it so I could support you. Besides, I found I naturally try to work in a collaborative way. Except when I have to be the big boss," Santa laughed.

"I serve the Workshop by being an icon. It gets a little tiring being 'larger than life,' but such is my responsibility. If I had handed you facilitation as the answer, I doubt we could scale this mountain. But now, I can see that you and your elves really believe that this is the path to the summit. Now that you believe in facilitation, we have a chance."

In the end, after much more discussion about the specifics of The Plan, Santa said that he could accept it as written. Rune felt a great sigh of relief knowing they had passed this major hurdle.

"Now, Rune," Santa said quietly, "tell me about your problems with Emil."

"I see you still are in touch with everything going on in the Workshop."

Santa's eyes twinkled. "It would be hard to miss this one. He's making quite a lot of noise. Even sending me e-mails every day, asking for an appointment. I replied to him that I was available next week."

"I'm sorry that this is taking your attention away from your other duties. Emil has been a supervisor in Wooden Toys for years. He very much values tradition. He has been troubled for some time with the changes we have been making, but this last effort has caused him deep anguish. He has been invited to participate in this process so he can share his views, but he continues to decline those invitations."

Santa sat quietly with a sad look on his face. "I know Emil. He is a good elf. He must be deeply troubled to take action like this. You mentioned that my memo had an impact on many of the elves. What effect do you think it had on him?"

"It appears to have had little effect on him. He has basically ignored it and discounts it when it is brought up to him. He has expressed skepticism about your knowledge about the details of this plan. He is bordering on insubordination."

"Given what you have told me, what do you think we should do?" Santa said, with an intent look on his face.

"I do not believe there is anything that can be done this weekend. Let us hold off on Emil until after Monday's meeting when we present The Plan. I believe that most of his support will ebb away once you put your stamp of approval on the specifics of this plan. Unless he takes some drastic action that requires our immediate response, I think there are advantages to letting this cool. It may be necessary for you to talk with Emil personally later. For the moment, I want to avoid a major confrontation with him. Let us leave room for him to back away from his position and preserve his honor. He is a valuable part of our Workshop community and I do not want to lose him."

Santa nodded his head in agreement. "I appreciate the respectful way you are handling this. There is a reason you are the right-hand elf to Santa Claus, my friend. You are a true elf. Your actions have been very consistent with traditional elfin values. I am sure that others in the Workshop are also noticing. I realize you are being put in a difficult position. But know how pleased I am with you. I have one more assignment for you this weekend. Don't work. Put all this aside. I need you fresh next week."

"Okay, Santa. Thanks for helping make this the best job in the world." Rune left Santa's office feeling like he was really going to get what he wanted for Christmas this year.

16

MONDAY
MORNING

23 WEEKS BEFORE
CHRISTMAS

The Big Meeting
with Santa

The last participant squeezed another chair around the table in Santa's office. All the elves were talking in hushed tones as they watched for Santa to move from his desk to the conference table.

Quiet fell over the room as he walked across the room. "Thank you for joining me today, especially the production managers. I am pleased to get together to review The Plan that so many of you have worked so hard to produce. This is a serious moment for the Workshop," Santa said, with his brow furrowed. "The children of the world are really at risk in so many ways, more than any time I can remember. A failure on our part would be devastating. Two weeks ago, I challenged Rune to come up with a plan to put us back on course for fulfilling our mission.

"I want to remind you that our task today is to review, modify (if necessary), and adopt a plan that will put the Workshop back on the right track. To get this done, we will have to stay focused on our task. On Friday, Rune walked me through a preliminary review. Overall, I am quite pleased with the content of The Plan. I assume all of you have studied it, too, so let's go right to the question-and-answer session."

Everyone in attendance had studied The Plan thoroughly. Santa joined them in asking questions of Rune, Pekka, and Helmi. Santa's staff was especially interested in how such a high level of participation was going to be achieved. The discussion was lively and the production managers took a lot of notes, scribbling madly in the margins while the discussion crackled around them.

"It's going to be really important that you make yourself very visible today, Santa," advised Urho. "That goes for you also, Rune. Elves are going to want to know what's going on and how our leaders are going to support this ambitious initiative. I strongly urge you to walk around the Workshop and talk with elves, at least through Wednesday."

"Thanks for the guidance, Urho," replied Rune. "I will be sure that everyone has a chance to see and talk with me."

"I'm happy to report that we updated our marketing model, so we should see improved stability in the forecast," offered Ragna.

"That is welcome news, Ragna," responded Rune. "Thank you for creating the new model. I hope the projections smooth out!"

Most of the time, Santa looked on during the discussion except when he added the observations that he had alluded to with Rune on Friday. A couple of times he refocused the attention of the group. When the conversation wound down, he cleared his throat quietly. Everyone noticed and looked to him.

"I am very pleased with this plan, not only because the content is solid but also because of the way it has been developed. Rune, it looks like you already have started the organization down a new path—one where facilitation is the norm and the level of participation of staff will increase dramatically. This will most assuredly help us produce the detailed action plan we need to reach our goal. The obvious differences in the quality of the working relationships are quite apparent. I congratulate all of you for that.

"If your elves ask, please quote Santa directly: *'I am in full support of this project.'* I believe it is necessary. Of course, I expect it to have a very positive effect on the Workshop. I am also aware that there are some in the Workshop who are against our moving forward on this. I hope they will give it their best try now that I am asking everyone to accept it. I want all of you to be as respectful as possible to each of them and make it easy for them to climb back into the fold. I also want you to be clear that there is no turning back.

"During the discussion, I did not hear any objection to the basic content of this plan. Isn't that right? Is there anyone here who has such strong reservations about this plan that you want us to reconsider it rather than adopting it?"

Santa looked around the room, stopping his gaze at every face. Every elf looked back at him without hesitation. "I need your commitment to publicly support this initiative. Do I have it?"

The elves around the table all nodded their heads in agreement.

Santa smiled at the result. "Thank you for that confirmation. We are about to undertake a process that will change the Workshop forever. This is a serious project that I expect will decide the fate of what we do here. Each one of us is going to have to give our hearts to its success or the Workshop will fail in its mission this year. To demonstrate that you are ready to commit to this plan and to the success of each other, I ask each of you join me now in the elfin tradition of contracting."

Chairs scratched across the hardwood floor as the production managers led all those in the room to their feet. Santa was the first to start shaking hands. He emotionally shook hands with Rune, Helmi, and Pekka. The production managers and Santa's staff all shook hands, too, acknowledging their commitment to the success of the project and each other.

"I thank you. We have a lot of work to do. Let's get at it." Santa slowly turned and strolled back to his desk.

Helped by the fact that all the elves were already on their feet, the room cleared within moments. As a group, the production managers made their way back to their work area. They paused by Rune's office.

"We have a good plan that each of you helped make better," said Rune. "You know your tasks and timing. Let's have a production managers meeting every Monday to review our progress and make any revisions necessary. Mean-

while, we need to quickly spread the word that Santa has en-
dorsed The Plan and we are to move quickly—full steam
ahead, as Pekka would say."

17

WEDNESDAY

MORNING

Rune and Pekka Meet with Emil

E mil," began Pekka, "thank you for coming in this morning. Would you like to join us in a cup of egg-nog before we start?"

Emil simply shook his head.

"I am sure you know why we have asked you to come here this morning," said Pekka quietly.

Emil looked directly at Pekka and then at Rune. "Why don't you tell me, since your voice mail only said that you wanted me here at nine."

Rune was amazed at Emil's continued defiance. As he had predicted, nearly all of Emil's support dwindled away when Santa walked around the Workshop endorsing The Plan. While many of these elves were still trying to understand what the changes would mean for them, they clearly saw that Santa meant business. Emil did not seem to understand the implications of his position.

"Emil, we haven't talked for a few days, and things have become much tougher for both of us because of that," continued Pekka, after a pause. "I'm still hoping that you will

understand the intention of this plan. You have much to
contribute to it and can even be a key player in helping us
implement it. Remember, we are trying to create a way for
every elf to have a say in what can be done to get these presents made. Even you have said the Workshop needs to make
some changes in order to succeed. I can really use your
help. This is about getting Santa's presents ready for the
children of the world. Won't you give me a hand, as you
used to do?"

Emil's face hardened as Pekka talked. "You are going to
wreck the Workshop, and it looks like there's nothing I can
do about it." Emil spat out the words. "It seems that you
and your gang of misguided managers has somehow fooled
Santa himself. I never thought that he would go along with
this disastrous plan. Tell me, Rune, how can you sleep at
night, knowing that you are betraying Santa Claus?"

"I sleep very well, thank you," replied Rune icily. "I am
going to explain this one more time although I do not have
much hope that you will hear my words. Emil, this is all
about helping the Workshop fulfill its mission. We want to
make some changes, but we wish to preserve what is good.
You are clearly an advocate for preserving our traditions
and values. We—"

"Save your breath, Rune. I have heard this speech so
many times that I could probably deliver it just as well as
you!" Emil's anger was beginning to boil.

"You might be able to repeat my words, but I don't
think you can hear me. Perhaps you can hear Santa." Rune

stood up and opened the door to the conference room. In walked Santa Claus.

"Hello, Emil. Hi, Rune, Pekka. Why don't the four of us have a little talk." Santa sat next to Emil. His kind, patient face warmed the room. The color had drained from Emil's face.

"Emil, I understand that you believe that I don't know the full story of what is happening in the Workshop and that you hope I will come to my senses and stop this change process. Is that right?"

Emil barely nodded his head in agreement.

"Emil, I know that working with me in the Workshop day in and day out can make me seem pretty ordinary. So I'd like to remind you of who I am. I'm the one who knows who's been bad and who's been good. I keep a list, remember? While it's true that keeping track of several million children does keep me busy, I save a little bit of energy for my favorite organization in the whole world, our Workshop.

"I have been watching you very closely this past couple of weeks, Emil. I read the memo you circulated that said, 'Santa does not fully understand what is going on, or he would never support such a plan.' Indeed! I don't recall assigning you the job as my spokes-elf, Emil." Santa laughed, but his piercing blue eyes held Emil's gaze.

"I am seriously concerned about reaching our goal this year. Two weeks ago, I charged Rune with developing a plan to get us back on track. To my delight, he and his team are choosing facilitation, a highly participative approach to solving this problem. But success is not about a 'magic plan.' It's about the elves who engage in the process and make it work. You can be a key player in that process, Emil. You can join in the exciting discussions that are taking place right now. Discussions about the very culture of the Workshop. Debates about what should change and what should remain the same.

"But you really have to believe in it, Emil. You have to believe that you can make a difference *and* that the Workshop is going to be successful—at least has a slim chance at it. If your heart tells you that you can help the Workshop by challenging our thinking and debating the changes, then please join us. But if your heart tells you that you just can't do this, then you'll need to leave the Workshop. It really has come to that."

Emil was shaking his head slowly. "I can't believe it's ending like this." He turned to Santa. "You say that I should follow my heart. My heart tells me that I no longer believe in Santa Claus." Tears were welling in Emil's eyes.

"Emil, I think we are all a bit tense right now," interjected Pekka. "Why don't you take a couple of days at home to think this over. Feel free to give any one of us a call. I really hope you change your mind. The team won't be the same without you."

Emil got up without a word and left the room. The meeting had devastated him, draining the last bit of hope from his heart. He returned to his office and sat at his desk for a while. Recovering somewhat from his shock, he slowly put all of his things in a plain brown box, carried them out to his sleigh, cracked the whip, and was gone. He never set foot in the Workshop again.

Friday morning, a courier delivered Emil's resignation letter to Santa, who called Rune and Pekka to his office shortly thereafter.

"Emil has decided to leave us. His letter is to me, and I am going to keep it confidential in his ER file. I will share the last line from it. 'Good luck, Santa, you are going to need it.' He's right, you know. The thing is, my little Workshop that produces millions of toys has a way of drawing good luck on a regular basis. It's because the love and generosity we share with the children of the world keeps sending good luck back to us. This has been a tough week already, my friends. I'm sorry we have lost Emil, but we have a lot of elves who are picking up the slack. Good luck, indeed!"

In the weeks to come, the phrase "Good Luck!" took on a special meaning for Pekka. Emil may not have intended it, but his final words to the Workshop served to inspire his old boss to become one of the most effective facilitators in the entire organization. Helmi's team came to request Pekka's presence in their work sessions. Their debates took on a new dimension of energy and creativity. And they got lucky a few times when their first attempt at a solution worked out. Good luck would soon shower down all over the Workshop.

18

A MONDAY MORNING IN SEPTEMBER | **15 WEEKS BEFORE CHRISTMAS**

Rune's Production Managers Meeting

I love the first real feeling of fall!" exclaimed Rune to the production managers gathered around the conference table. "I find the crispness of the air so invigorating! Plus, I know it is not yet time to panic—there is only a little snow in the air."

Helmi spoke up. "The numbers must be good this week. Anytime Rune starts off this meeting with a weather report, I know that's a good sign." The others laughed out loud.

"This year has been about as predictable as the weather," responded Veli. "Remember the last week in July? Going to that production meeting felt like a march to a funeral."

Sigrid grimaced at the memory. "We tried to do so much! It was nearly our undoing to create changes at all levels of the organization while trying to produce at full capacity. That near freeze in production lasted far longer than any of us imagined it would. Those last two weeks of July racked up a bunch of zeros for production. Nothing much was produced as the elves were talking about what and how to change."

"Once we got going, though, we really picked up speed," added Sisko. "We had so many good ideas come out of our process. I am still amazed at how quickly they were evaluated and implemented. I couldn't believe how totally involved my elves were. Some of my team members told me that this has been the highlight of their careers."

Rune studied the papers in front of him while he overheard the discussions going on around the room. This experience was far different from the meetings back in June and July. Helmi and Sisko were talking about events in their personal lives. Even Sigrid, who was the quietest member of the team, was engaged in an animated conversation with Veli. Rune realized that his managers were more involved with each other. The focus on work had been a constant. But to experience the group members caring about one another was rewarding. Rune was sure that the quality of the working relationships among his staff was contributing to their success.

"What sticks out in my mind," said Helmi, "was how the managers and supervisors quickly learned the value of facilitation. So many of them are using it every day. I see charts in their offices reminding them of the three steps. They really adjusted their work styles. They picked up on the philosophy, the model, and the tools. With all of us operating in this new way, the momentum built really fast. And because we were focused on *both* getting the work done *and* working together more effectively, we were able to stay focused. Speaking of facilitation, where's our 'Power Facilitator,' Pekka?"

"He asked my permission to be fifteen minutes late," responded Rune. "The assembly re-engineering team asked him to facilitate its early morning meeting. Since we are taking a moment to reflect, there was one area that surprised me. I did not think we would need to spend so much time defining what it means to be an elf in the Workshop. I am proud of the work we did on clarifying key elfin values. Some of our less experienced elves reported that they felt listened to and understood for the first time. And our most experienced elves are innovating like never before. I know that the Workshop has the capability to achieve our goal. And we still have a long way to go.

"Hello, Pekka! How did your meeting go?"

"It went really well, Rune," responded Pekka. "Veli, I'll need to go over some things with you after this meeting."

"Let us get started," interrupted Rune. "I was just noticing that our team is changing, just as the entire Workshop is changing. Our working relationships have improved. I sense more energy in our group, in spite of the rapid pace we have had to work at. We are more connected to each other. It is a personal dividend that I had not expected."

FACILITATION STEPS

1. Help others take responsibility.

2. Help others focus on what they need to get done.

3. Help improve working relationships.

"I have thought about this a lot," said Pekka. "Before this summer, I felt much more distant from everyone else in this group. I just focused on my part of the Workshop and assumed all the other managers were taking care of their responsibilities. Now, I feel connected with all of you. Before, I judged Helmi to be a competitor who was jockeying for position. She has since become one of my most trusted colleagues. We still have great debates, but they are debates that help us achieve common goals. I have observed other elves around the Workshop being more supportive and trusting of one another. And the arguments are as spirited as ever! So I believe our team is mirroring what is happening across the whole organization."

"You're right, Pekka," responded Helmi. "They really do watch us and take their cues from us. That's why it was so much fun in our meeting the other day when you admitted *in public* that I had convinced you to change your mind about the new work flow system. I wish I had videotaped that!"

Everyone laughed. Then a thoughtful silence enveloped them all as they enjoyed the levity of this moment.

After a while, Rune spoke up. "We have some encouraging production numbers to review this morning. We are not out of the woods yet, but I have confidence that we will make it. And I cannot imagine going on this journey with any other elves. Now, about those numbers."

Everyone turned to look at the chart Rune placed on the easel. Their faces depicted a range of emotions that changed as they looked at different elements of the chart.

"If you look at the production report, you will see what I am talking about. We have doubled our productivity since July. That is an amazing recovery. Reaching the September new goal puts us in a position to achieve our mission. I offer a qualified 'congratulations' to all of us. I encourage all of you to share this information with your staffs."

The team cheered the news, smiles beaming all around.

"I also want to remind you," continued Rune, "that our new goals for October, November, and December are significantly higher than September's. So we have some serious work ahead of us."

19

A MONDAY
MORNING LATE
IN NOVEMBER

4 WEEKS BEFORE
CHRISTMAS

Rune's Production Managers Meeting

I can feel the momentum!" proclaimed Rune. He looked positively gleeful. "I believe we are actually going to do it! Look at these results." With that, Rune handed out copies of the latest production report. "We not only have caught up with our lost production, but we are now ahead of our targets. The thing that gave us this last boost was our improvement in quality. With fewer production problems, our scrap is down to almost nothing. We have closed the gap. We have a lot of work to do in this last month but I think we are going to make it!"

"At this point, I feel relief more than I feel like celebrating," responded Pekka. "I don't know about the rest of you, but I am fried. Still, it feels good to be so close to victory."

"Relaxation in January—I can see a warm tropical island in my future," said Helmi.

"Helmi, do you want me to facilitate a planning session for your vacation?" asked Sigrid.

"No. I think I'll just show up and see what happens."

"I am glad to hear you planning your celebrations," said Rune. "We have four weeks to go, so let's make sure we run hard past the finish line." Rune felt both confident and cautious as he addressed the group. "I remember when all of us were doing some soul-searching about our bleak prospects. I certainly had my doubts. But we persevered, and we sit here today on the verge of reaching the peak of this mountain."

Helmi nodded in agreement. "Let's look at those production numbers again."

"Before we do that—I'm feeling a bit reflective, too," added Pekka. "I know that we are all tired. Relaxation in January will be just the ticket for me and, I am sure, most elves at the Workshop. Yet this is a point we need to celebrate. This is a really big deal and we are pulling it off. This has been hard! Everyone is to be congratulated."

Sisko commented, "I, for one, had begun to prepare myself for the ugly reality of our failing. At times, I felt like I was going through the motions of trying to make it all work out. Even with our improvements, I have been fearing something would blindside us again. Now I can see that we even have some excess capacity to handle any last-minute glitches. I am trying to get my heart restarted from the shock of what has happened. Maybe I should ask Santa for a defibrillator for Christmas."

Veli looked around the table a moment. "I want to say how much I appreciate the leadership provided by Rune, Helmi, and Pekka. The three of you were able to create a vision of how we could work together differently and find solutions that would otherwise have eluded us. You gave substance to the nice words you were using. You really led by example. I kept watching as you struggled but kept working together. You really did use your differences as assets rather than liabilities. I think 'helping others take responsibility, focus on what they need to get done, and improve their working relationships' is now permanently imprinted on my brain. I am proud to be an elf in this Workshop. I salute you!"

"And before you say, 'We couldn't have done it without everyone else,'" injected Sigrid, "hear our appreciation for you. We know we could not have done it without you. I know that I am speaking on behalf of those in this room and around the Workshop. We all had to work together to achieve what these numbers represent. Everyone did their part. You led the way. You are awesome leaders."

"Thank you," said Rune quietly. "I am deeply touched, especially in light of the fears we all have overcome."

"Thank you," Pekka and Helmi said nearly in unison. There was laughter all around the table.

"I guess we are finally beginning to think alike," said Helmi, with another laugh.

"I wouldn't go that far," retorted Pekka. "But I have learned a lot from you. I have come to respect and appreciate you, which is a dramatic shift from where I was six months ago."

Rune smiled with deep satisfaction. "I think we all have learned so much during these past few months. I do not want us to lose that. How about if we spend a few minutes documenting what we have learned? Helmi and Pekka, could you cofacilitate the discussion?"

They spent the balance of the meeting identifying the lessons that they had learned. When the meeting broke up, the elves had a noticeable bounce in their steps. They were all enjoying the rewards of having worked hard, of having the goal in sight. The managers recorded the lessons they had learned, and Rune made sure that every elf got a copy.

LESSONS LEARNED

Facilitation is helping elves get their work done and improve the way they work together.

- Facilitation is a supporting role, focused on helping others succeed in their work.
- When a facilitator is also a manager or leader, it helps to be clear which role you are fulfilling at the moment. Otherwise, elves get confused.
- Focusing on the task at hand helps elves be more comfortable as they explore their working relationships.

The nature of facilitation includes

- Valuing the contributions of all.
- Believing that collaboration creates better results.
- Assuming that differences among people is a required part of collaboration.
- Helping others achieve results by expressing themselves productively and taking action.

The steps of facilitation

Helping others take responsibility

- It is much easier to take responsibility for tasks when they are clearly tied to the mission.
- Taking mutual responsibility is not the same as delegating.
- Taking responsibility is taking ownership of the results.

Helping others focus on what they need to get done

- Focusing on the task at hand is the key to being productive.
- When tension is high, it is easy to get off track. Often, clearly restating the task at hand helps everyone reorient themselves.

Helping others improve their working relationships

- Elves are increasingly dependent on each other. Poor relationships make success harder to achieve.
- Committing to one another's success is key to achieving the goal.
- The context of a relationship is the work that elves do together.
- When the task is the focus, it is easier to talk about behaviors and feelings.

20

CHRISTMAS

EVE

The Celebration at the Launching Pad of Santa's Sleigh

The snow was falling softly all around Santa's Workshop as the elves gathered on the big, round launching pad for Santa's sleigh. The huge bag on the back of the sleigh was bulging with presents. Santa had his customary Christmas smile drawn up like a bow. His cheeks were already rosy and the elves could hear him laughing softly. The core of the warp drive was glowing a soft green and the Time Slice Multiplexor computers were humming quietly. The reindeer were in their traces and pawing at the snow in eagerness to get on with their journey. Rudolph was at the front, his nose aglow and a bright look in his eyes.

This was the moment the elves looked forward to each year. This year, it had an even more special meaning since so many of them had thought they would never get everything finished in time. But they had done it! All the presents were on the sleigh, wrapped and labeled for each child around the world.

Now, as they gave their attention to the outside world, the elves could see that the children needed Santa now more than ever. With war and political upheaval creating fear and poverty on every continent, children were desperately in need of the unconditional love and care that Santa delivered to them every Christmas Eve.

As was their elfin tradition, Santa went back into the Workshop to retrieve his special bag of presents for the elves. He always did this just before departing. Giving them their gifts then was his way of rewarding them for their hard work over the year. They waited for him now, knowing he would be carrying his big bag when he appeared. These presents were so very valuable because Santa had made them himself especially for every elf in the Workshop. Each gift would somehow be exactly what the elf wanted or perfect in some other way.

Everyone fell silent as the gentle tinkling of bells could be heard. All eyes were drawn to the door. Suddenly it swept open and Santa bounced into sight with a huge bag across his shoulder.

He had a big smile and a twinkle in his eye, and everyone heard his voice. "Ho! Ho! Ho! Merry Christmas to all who have made this the most wonderful Christmas yet for so many children around the world!" With that, he began to pass out his presents from the bag that never seemed to empty. Everywhere he went, the elves felt their spirits soar. When he was finished, he hopped up onto his sleigh and faced the crowd.

"Thank you from the bottom of my heart. You have embodied the Christmas spirit all this past year. You did it! You climbed the tallest mountain we have ever faced. You beat insurmountable odds. The thought of your dedication, your skill, your will to win will carry me through the night!

"Before I leave, I want to call particular attention to the one elf that has made the biggest difference. The work that he and his team did this past year is truly magical. He helped us create anew Santa's Workshop, the most amazing place to work on this entire earth. He led us through a complex series of changes. And let's not forget that we are the world's largest manufacturing facility, bar none. Through all of that, he helped us preserve, and in some ways rediscover, what it means to be an elf, supporting this Workshop, making the world a better place for children. He embodies the values we associate with Christmas. He showed us how to stay close to our values, even as we embarked on changing the Workshop in fundamental ways. He led by example. He facilitated some very sticky situations. All of you are to be congratulated because I could not have started my rounds tonight without every one of you doing your part. But I ask you all to join me now in saluting Rune."

With that, the elves burst into wild cheering and applause. Rune bowed to them all, remembering his elf manners.

With a wave of his hand, Santa began his final preparations. The elves watched him and felt a satisfaction deeper than they had ever known. They had done it and they were proud of themselves. This was a successful Christmas!

Then, in the early evening darkness, a hush fell over all the elves. They knew the moment of departure was near. As the sleigh began to slowly rise from the snow, the elves let out an enormous cheer. From high above, they could hear the familiar voice: *"Happy Christmas to all, and to all a good-night!"*

Notes

1. http://mud.primenet.com/tfc/history/elf.html
   (accessed September 28, 2002); "Elves, Goblins,
   and Others," http://ashvital.freeservers.com/elves,
   %20goblins%20and%20others.htm (accessed
   September 28, 2002).
2. "Christmas Elves," http://www.didyouknow.cd/xmas/
   xmaselves.htm (accessed September 28, 2002); "The
   History of Santa Claus," http://www.the-north-pole.
   com/history/ (accessed September 28, 2002).

About the Authors

Dr. Richard G. Weaver and John D. Farrell are internationally recognized for their expertise in facilitation. For nearly ten years, they have worked together helping organizations use facilitation to achieve their goals. They have helped a number of groups and teams succeed in challenging situations. A key element of this process has been helping team leaders and others in organizations learn to facilitate more effectively. John and Richard have worked with organizations in Africa, Asia, eastern and western Europe, and North and South America. They have written two books together: *Managers as Facilitators: A Practical Guide to Getting Work Done in a Changing Workplace,* Berrett-Koehler Publishers (1997) and *The Practical Guide to Facilitation: A Self-Study Resource,* Berrett-Koehler Publishers and Human Resources Development Press (2000).

Richard G. Weaver has been facilitating for forty years, professionally for nearly thirty-five years. He is internationally recognized as a facilitator and author as well as a consultant, speaker, trainer, teacher, and executive coach. He has an extensive background in organizational dynamics that he uses in his work in organizations, his teaching, and his writing. He makes a clear link between the theoretical and the practical. Dr. Weaver has worked with groups and individuals from California to Washington, D.C., to the Middle East and Africa. He has done significant facilitation work with clients such as NCR, AMOCO Production Company, AT&T, and Chrysler Corporation.

His rich work history has included working in social agencies, working in businesses, running his own consulting firm called New Possibilities, and teaching undergraduates and graduates. (He is currently teaching at the University of California, Irvine.) Intertwined with these work responsibilities, Dr. Weaver has earned a master's degree in counseling (University of Dayton), a master's degree in business administration (Wright State University), and a doctorate in human and organizational systems (The Fielding Graduate Institute).

John D. Farrell has been facilitating professionally for fifteen years. He is internationally recognized as an executive, consultant, and author as well as a speaker, trainer, and executive coach. He has an extensive background in organization development that he uses in his work as an executive and in his writing. Mr. Farrell has worked with groups and individuals across North America, eastern and western Europe, and South America. He has had significant facilitation work with clients such as AT&T, NCR, and numerous government agencies at the state and federal level.

His rich work history has included working in industries such as food manufacturing (the Pillsbury Company), chemicals (Dow Corning Corporation), consulting (Deloitte Consulting), and software development (Ontrack Data International). Mr. Farrell has a bachelor of science degree in chemical engineering (University of Illinois) and has completed the International Organization and System Development program through the Gestalt Institute of Cleveland and the Institute fur Gestaltorientierte Organisationsberatung in Frankfurt.

Visit www.facilitationsource.com for more information on facilitation and the authors.

Berrett-Koehler Publishers

Berrett-Koehler is an independent publisher of books and other publications at the leading edge of new thinking and innovative practice on work, business, management, leadership, stewardship, career development, human resources, entrepreneurship, and global sustainability.

Since the company's founding in 1992, we have been committed to creating a world that works for all by publishing books that help us to integrate our values with our work and work lives, and to create more humane and effective organizations.

We have chosen to focus on the areas of work, business, and organizations, because these are central elements in many people's lives today. Furthermore, the work world is going through tumultuous changes, from the decline of job security to the rise of new structures for organizing people and work. We believe that change is needed at all levels—individual, organizational, community, and global— and our publications address each of these levels.

To find out about our new books,
special offers,
free excerpts,
and much more,
subscribe to our free monthly eNewsletter at

www.bkconnection.com

The Power of Appreciative Inquiry

Diana Whitney and Amanda Trosten-Bloom

The Power of Appreciative Inquiry is a comprehensive and practical guide to using Appreciative Inquiry for strategic large-scale change. Written by pioneers in the field, the book provides detailed examples along with practical guidance for using AI in an organizational setting.

Paperback, 264 pages • ISBN 1-57675-226-7
Item #52267 $27.95

Managers As Mentors
Building Partnerships for Learning

Chip R. Bell

Managers As Mentors is a provocative guide to helping associates grow and adapt in today's tumultuous organizations. Chip Bell persuasively shows that today mentoring means valuing creativity over control, fostering growth by facilitating learning, and helping others get smart, not just get ahead. His hands-on, down-to-earth advice takes the mystery out of effective mentoring, teaching leaders to be the confident coaches integral to learning organizations.

Paperback, 206 pages • ISBN 1-57675-034-5
Item #50345 $18.95

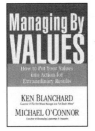

Managing By Values

Ken Blanchard and Michael O'Connor

Based on over 25 years of research and application, *Managing By Values* provides a practical game plan for defining, clarifying, and communicating an organization's values and ensuring that its practices are in line with those values throughout the organization.

Paperback, 160 pages • ISBN 1-57675-274-7
Item #52747 $14.95

Berrett-Koehler Publishers
PO Box 565, Williston, VT 05495-9900
Call toll-free! **800-929-2929** 7 am-9 pm EST
Or fax your order to 802-864-7627
For fastest service order online: **www.bkconnection.com**